Praise for

READBACK

"Becoming a United States Marine Corps officer is hard enough, and even more difficult is becoming a pilot in a USMC light attack squadron where everyone is top-notch. Within this context, readers will find the advice and wisdom contained throughout these pages invaluable. Ryan's "Readbacks" at the end of each chapter are priceless lessons for anyone navigating the executive business world or life's many challenges."

LT. GEN. STEVEN "STICK" RUDDER, USMC (ret.)

"Leadership is truly an art. Instead of ink, oils, clay, or chords, a leader must work with people and relationships to build the teamwork and trust necessary to achieve the intangible, but real, esprit de corps that drives individuals and organizations to excel beyond their expectations. In *Readback*, Ryan Cherry uses his unique and insightful real-life experiences to communicate the art and science of inspiring people in a way anyone can relate to. Your mind will race as you apply these pages to scenarios from your own life. Through the lessons in this book, you'll become the type of leader that others will not just want to follow but to become themselves."

LT. GEN. LANCE "SPIKE" LANDRUM, USAF (ret.), President and Founder of Team Landrum Advising & Consulting LLC

"*Readback* is a masterclass in resilience, drawn from the skies of combat and the quiet battles of everyday life. Ryan Cherry's journey as a Marine Cobra pilot is more than an adrenaline-filled story—it's a guide to facing fear, embracing discipline, and turning adversity into your fuel for success. It's about life, leadership, and pushing through when things get tough. Whether you're chasing a goal, leading a team, or just trying to level up in life, this book will push you to dig deeper, aim higher, and never back down."

COL. EVERETT "FINGERS" GOOD, USMC, Commanding Officer of Marine Aircraft Group 29

"I have known Ryan for many years and first met him at the time I commanded Marine Aircraft Group 39. This book, a compilation of personal experiences which led to the development and maturing of his personal leadership philosophy, is a unique approach to selflessly imparting valuable lessons learned for others to incorporate into their own developing leadership styles. I believe, 'It is good to learn from your own mistakes, but it is far easier to learn from the mistakes of others.' Ryan does a masterful job of detailing the good and not-so-good experiences of his life to assist those who follow him in their own leadership progression."

COL. PATRICK "PADDY" GOUGH, USMC (ret), CEO of Poseidon Consulting LLC

"A must-read for all new or aspiring junior officers, noncommissioned officers, and civilian front line leaders."

COL. TIM HORAN, USA (ret.), Former President of National Grid Rhode Island

"*Readback* is a thought-provoking blend of hard-fought lessons in leadership set against the operations of our modern military. Every leader in every industry will level up with this uniquely personal look at a distinguished career and the leadership lessons learned along the way. Colonel Cherry details both his successes and his mistakes—all to our benefit. Sure, you can learn leadership skills from entrepreneurs and CEOs, but few of them have made decisions that are actual life and death. *Readback* is a reminder that as leaders, our choices matter, our people matter, and our teams will never perform better than what we are personally capable of."

SEAN DEVEREAUX, Film Producer, Founder, Entrepreneur

READBACK

A MARINE AVIATOR'S MANUAL *for* Navigating Life's Hardest Lessons

RYAN A. CHERRY
Colonel, USMC (Ret.)

www.amplifypublishinggroup.com

Readback: A Marine Aviator's Manual for Navigating Life's Hardest Lessons

For more information, please contact:
Amplify Publishing, an imprint of Amplify Publishing Group
620 Herndon Parkway, Suite 220
Herndon, VA 20170
info@amplifypublishing.com

Library of Congress Control Number: 2025926050

CPSIA Code: PRV1125A

ISBN-13: 979-8-89138-855-0

Printed in United States

To my son, Joey—I started writing this book to give you a glimpse inside my head; a look at who I am as a Marine and what's important to me as your father. Thank you for the inspiration and the joy you bring to me and Mom. This book is for you. I love you!

CONTENTS

Why I Wrote This Book

I wrote this book to share concepts I wish I had understood before having to learn them the hard way.

For years, I have taken note of the significant lessons I've learned along the way, lessons that had impact on me and my life. Memories of events that served as "aha" moments. I didn't want to forget them.

As each memory popped into my head, I would begin to ponder it; I considered how the event happened, how I reacted, and how a problem was resolved or wasn't. To prevent each lesson from departing my mind as quickly as it had entered—a problem we all have as we grow older—I started to capture the ideas in the Notes page of my iPhone.

As the list grew, I would occasionally recall something my boss, Lieutenant General John Toolan, would say to me when I was his

Aide-de-Camp* at Marine Forces Pacific. When something important, strange, challenging, or funny would happen, he would tell me to "put it in the book." At the time, and until I started contemplating *this* book, I would laugh at the thought of *me* writing a book. Who am I to write a book?

Only in the past few years did the idea start to grow within me. I'm approaching retirement from the Marine Corps and pondering what's next for me. I finally realized I needed to get these memories, my lessons learned, out of my head and onto paper.

I'm writing while still on active duty. When I started, I was about a year and a half away from retiring from the Marine Corps as a Colonel. For Christmas, I asked my wife for a Bluetooth keyboard and mouse to go along with my old Dell computer. I wake up between 0400 and 0430 every weekday morning to spend thirty to sixty minutes writing before my workday begins.

As I write, I'm struggling with the same question I had as Lieutenant General Toolan's Aide: Who am I to write a book and what will readers, if I have any, get from it? Who am I writing for, anyway?

For now, I'm writing for myself. Getting these ideas on the page is therapeutic for me. Like most Marines, I'd like to tell myself I don't have mental health issues but that would be a lie.

I'm also writing for my family, most importantly my son, Joey. If he is the only person who reads these pages, the time spent writing this will have been worth every minute, every 0400 wake up. I want Jenny (my wife), Joey, and the rest of my family to understand

---

* Aide-de-Camp: A military officer serving as a confidential assistant to a high-ranking military officer who is responsible for assisting the senior officer in the performance of their duties.

who I am, what has shaped me, and why I act the way I do; to do that, I have to let them get a glimpse inside my head, so here it is.

The words I'm writing also go out to Marines and other service members, because I sure wish I had learned these lessons before I had to live them. Hearing or reading these twenty-two lessons before I had to experience them in real life would have helped prepare me for the challenges to come, and I'm hoping it will help other service members, too.

If you've been in the Marine Corps or another military branch for a long time, you'll recognize yourself in these pages. You have probably already learned many of these lessons to one degree or another, but that doesn't mean you can't still benefit—in fact, I expect you'll connect more deeply to the lessons offered here. And if you're new to the Marine Corps, or military service, this book may help you sidestep a few pitfalls or provide a springboard to success when you're faced with the challenges that will inevitably come your way.

Finally, I'm writing for civilians who have never served, whether they are thinking about serving or not.

This book is for anyone who is looking for ways to succeed in challenging times. The takeaways I've captured here can help you succeed on any path you choose.

Who I Am

Events unique to your life shape you into the person you are today. Each new event adds an ingredient into the recipe of who you will become. It's the same for me: I'm a product of where I'm from, who raised me, my unique experiences, and my DNA. This is my story.

My parents were raised in Pawtucket, Rhode Island. Both came from lower- to lower-middle-class families and grew up steeped in the culture and understanding of the post-WWII generation. Mom was a schoolteacher and Dad enlisted in the Marine Corps during the Vietnam draft because he couldn't find a way to pay for college.

High school sweethearts, they were married after Dad's graduation from boot camp. They were both extremely hard workers who always found a way to move forward to the next step in life. As a newlywed couple, they persevered and overcame the challenges of Vietnam and the transition to postwar life in America—returning home, transitioning to civilian life, and starting a family back in Rhode Island.

Dad worked his way up the management ladder of a local machinist company called Brown & Sharpe in North Kingstown, Rhode Island, and would become a vice president for a Johnson & Johnson company. He also started his own business with Mom while being promoted to Chief Warrant Officer 4 as a reservist drilling in the Marine Corps.

Mom was a teacher and the backbone of my parents' entrepreneurial adventure, "Military Fashion," a mail-order clothing store. While raising me and my two brothers, she moved on from teaching but dove into volunteering in many organizations, most importantly every school the three of us boys attended. She was in a position to watch, raise, assist, and discipline as needed. You would think the Marine dad would be the disciplinarian, but a Marine's wife is often the most frightening person to encounter when you've chosen to do the wrong thing. (She was also the one to unintentionally teach us all the really good swear words. Thanks, Mom!)

By "us" I mean me and my two older brothers, Jonathan and Jason. It's a certainty that we are a lot alike. We all look like we are our father's sons, and we all carry common characteristics of both parents.

My brothers both found wonderful women to marry, have amazing children, and have found success in their chosen fields. Jon, my oldest brother, is a successful PhD working in the business world and Jay is in finance, highly sought after as a CFO for any company looking to improve their bottom line.

Like my brothers, I'm a combination of the traits of my parents, though my likes and talents are different from theirs. I've got Dad's drive, business savvy, willingness to help others in need, loyalty, and sharp edges. These are mixed with Mom's work ethic, love of life and those who are closest to her, and kindness (unless she was on the "War Path"*). That's the "starter pack" for who I am today, with an emphasis on Dad's sharp edges; thankfully, these are sheathed by the kindness and love of others I got from Mom.

Each of us, in our own way, has become what our parents wanted us to be.

I was born in Pawtucket, Rhode Island; we started out in Central Falls, moved to North Kingstown, and ended up spending most of my childhood in Mansfield, Massachusetts. Elementary school was difficult for me and shaped many of my character traits, or, more specifically, cemented some of my internal insecurities.

* War Path: A term used to describe my mom's actions when we had pushed her too far or weren't listening. Her tactics were genius; she didn't need to yell or be outwardly angry. Her War Path was filled with a quiet intensity devoid of the extra care and feeding we were so lucky to have from her.

When I was in second grade, my Aunt Liz discovered I had hearing loss. To this point no one had noticed my hearing problem. I could hear what I was paying attention to, but if I was not focused on something, I wasn't able to hear the world around me. I had missed so much that by the time I reached third grade, I felt like I was starting school all over again. I understand this is only my perspective as a little kid, but it is fairly accurate. I was playing catch-up with my classmates, learning many of the lessons I should have learned in first and second grade. (My hearing problem was resolved with a few rounds of "tubes" in my ears, and my hearing is perfect now, even after twenty-plus years of flying helicopters.)

In third grade, I found myself having to leave the regular classroom, going to the resource room for extra help. This program would save me, but it was very difficult to accept as a kid. For most of the reading time in elementary school, the kids were broken up into groups. Each group was filled with kids at the same level of reading. Some groups were called the Blue Jays or the Robins. I felt like I was put in the Dirt Squirrels reading group.

I took two good things and two bad things away from this early life experience. The first good thing was the extra help I received as a Dirt Squirrel got me back in step with my peers and helped me surpass many by seventh grade. Next, I found my lifelong best friend—Stephen Nangle. He was a Dirt Squirrel for different reasons, but we were able to commiserate over our station in life and share our understanding that we were not really supposed to be there . . .

The two negative things I keep to this day are baked into who I am. First, I had a paralyzing fear of reading aloud. In grade school, I would attempt to read ahead of the class as each person read their section with the hope of being able to read my section ahead of time. I'm sure others did the same thing, but I would have mini panic attacks (I had no idea what a panic attack was as a kid) while stumbling and stammering through my turn to read. Even knowing how to read and read well, I couldn't get through my part without feeling like my heart and lungs would explode.

I still hate to read aloud! I can give a speech in front of hundreds of people. I can brief a flight and provide updates to three- and four-star Generals without any issues. But give me a promotion warrant or award and my insides begin to turn. I don't know for certain, but I think my deep-seated fear of reading aloud goes back to the stupid kid in elementary school who couldn't hear and had to leave the room with the rest of the Dirt Squirrels.

The second negative is an internal voice that tells me I'm not good enough. The voice tells me if it's too hard, I can't do it. This voice will not allow me to put myself out there, in public, as someone who is better than anyone else. Even when my career has shown that I am better than many in most cases and better than everyone in a select few instances.

The internal voice also tells me if I *can* do something, it can't be difficult. If I can do it, anyone can do it. It doesn't matter what I've accomplished—being a captain on my high school football team, playing football in college (D3), graduating Officer Candidate School (OCS),* completing The Basic School (TBS),† getting a flight

---

* Officer Candidate School (OCS): A ten-week training program for aspiring Marine Corps Officers located in Quantico, Virginia.

† The Basic School (TBS): A six-month school for all newly commissioned Marine Corps Officers.

contract,[*] finishing first in flight school (in the top 1 percent to ever graduate), getting my first choice of aircraft, surviving combat, finding my person (Jenny), getting command of a squadron, getting promoted to Colonel—if I've done it, I figure it was no big deal. Even though each of these things is extremely difficult and most people have little to no chance of accomplishing even one of them, never mind all of them. But in my head, once I've completed something difficult, I discount it right away. If a Dirt Squirrel can do it, anyone can. Right?

As I approached high school graduation, I told my dad I was thinking about enlisting in the Marine Corps. His response was fairly straightforward: He told me if I tried to enlist, he would "break my f'ing legs." At the time, I really thought he meant it too.

He had enlisted in the Marine Corps during the Vietnam draft. He couldn't pay to go to college, and he had few options available to him. After transitioning to the Reserves,[†] he made it to the rank of Gunnery Sergeant before becoming a Warrant Officer. Having seen the Marine Corps from both the enlisted and officer sides, he felt fortunate to be an officer. Still, he wanted to give me something his parents would not, or could not, give him. He was driven to put all of his boys through college and send us into the world without the debt many people are saddled with.

In the end, he told me that if I wanted to be a Marine, I could be a Marine with a college degree.

---

* Flight Contract: A guaranteed opportunity to attend flight school to become a Naval Aviator in the Marine Corps.

† Reserve Marine Corps: Trained Marines who support the active Marine Corps in times of war, national emergencies, and other contingencies. In peacetime, Marine Reservists train one weekend a month and two weeks a year.

I chose to go to Springfield College in Western Massachusetts. Springfield College is the birthplace of basketball and had notable students like Don Ho and John Cena. However, the most important graduate was Jennifer Leigh Haschig. There are far too many things I could say about this gorgeous and wonderful lady who would become my wife, too many to capture here . . . maybe another book?

I played football in college. I didn't have the Marine Corps physique then; I was an offensive and defensive lineman. I was six feet, three inches tall and weighed in at about 250 pounds. I studied rehabilitation services, a strange major that would have allowed me to be a social worker or a doctor. My intent was to become a physical therapist, had I not joined the Marine Corps.

Career

My fate was sealed one November afternoon when I came across an Officer Selection Officer (OSO)* during my junior year in college. An OSO is a USMC recruiter for officers. Captain Bennet Walsh had a booth set up in the student common area. I walked up to him and asked what I had to do to become a Marine Cobra helicopter pilot. He smiled, asked me a few questions, and handed me his card, telling me to come see him in his office.

I made an appointment to meet with him. Shortly after, I went into the OSO office, filled out some paperwork, and sat down to talk to Captain Walsh. He was professional and to the point: He told me that if I wanted to be a Marine, I had to lose some weight

---

* Officer Selection Officer (OSO): A Marine recruiter responsible for finding qualified individuals to attend Officers Candidate School and commission as Second Lieutenants.

first. I remember him putting it this way: "Lose some weight and we can talk."

I was hooked! (I was also offended; it was a total slap in the face.) Clearly, this OSO didn't need me; if I wanted to be a Marine, to be someone, to be like my dad, I'd have to meet his challenge. I'd have to prove myself.

The weight loss was fairly simple. To maintain my football weight, I had been eating a *lot* of food. I just needed to start eating a normal diet and running and the weight melted away. About a month later, I was back in the OSO's office, down about twenty pounds. I was ready to start my Marine Corps journey.

My package to go to OCS was complete and I passed the Aviation Selection Test Battery.* Passing this test guaranteed me a spot in flight school. The path to become a Cobra pilot was going to be hard, but I had taken my first steps.

And then I took off running.

I completed OCS during the summer of 1999, between my junior and senior years. I was commissioned as a Second Lieutenant on the USS *Constitution*, "Old Ironsides," in Boston Harbor the day before I graduated college. I completed TBS in the spring of 2001 and was in flight school on September 11, 2001. I did well enough in flight school to get my first choice,† AH-1W Cobra helicopters at Camp Pendleton, in Oceanside, California.

---

* Aviation Selection Test Battery: The primary test used by the US Navy, Marine Corps, and Coast Guard for the selection of officer aviation program applicants to receive a flight contract and attend flight school.

† First choice: When I completed flight school, graduates selected their airframe one at a time, from highest score to lowest score. The type of aircraft and duty stations available for selection were written on a whiteboard. The first person walked into the room and picked what they wanted and the last person walked into the room picked the only option remaining.

I spent my first six years in the fleet with Marine Light Attack Helicopter Squadron 369 (HMLA-369), the "Gunfighters."* During that time, I earned every designation and qualification I could, including Night Systems Instructor (NSI)† and Weapons and Tactics Instructor (WTI).‡ These qualifications were important, because they gave me the Military Occupational Specialty (MOS)§ credibility I needed to get promoted.

During my first Fleet tour, I deployed five times: four deployments to Iraq and one deployment to Okinawa, Japan, as part of the Unit Deployment Program (UDP).¶

After my first tour in the Gunfighters, I had a short stint in a new unit called Marine Aviation Training Systems Site (MATSS)** at Camp Pendleton before being promoted to Major and selected to attend the Naval War College in Newport, Rhode Island, for

---

* Marine Light Attack Helicopter Squadron (HMLA): A composite squadron of Marine AH-1 attack and UH-1 utility helicopters.

† Night Systems Instructor (NSI): An NSI is qualified to instruct students during syllabus events at night.

‡ Weapons and Tactics Instructor (WTI): A seven-week course of instruction in Yuma, Arizona combining all functions of Marine Corps aviation to create the highest quality aviators. A Squadron WTI holds the highest instructor qualifications in the squadron and is responsible for developing and executing the training plan for Marine Corps squadrons.

§ Military Occupational Specialty (MOS): A code that designates a Marine in a specific job or military specialty.

¶ Unit Deployment Program (UDP): A Marine Corps program that rotates US-based squadrons on six-month deployments to the Western Pacific.

** Marine Aviation Training Systems Site (MATSS): A facility that provides aviation and maintenance simulation and training.

Intermediate Level School (ILS),[*] a major stepping stone for promotion as an officer in the Marine Corps.

Then it was off to Hawaii to join HMLA-367, "Scarface." During our three years in Hawaii, I served as the Operations Officer (OpsO)[†] for Scarface, the Detachment Officer in Charge (Det OIC)[‡] of the skid det (Cobra and Huey detachment) on the 31st Marine Expeditionary Unit (MEU),[§] and as the Aide-de-Camp for the Marine Forces Pacific Commander, Lieutenant General John Toolan.

Next up, orders to the Pentagon to join the Headquarters Marine Corps (HQMC) Operations Directorate, Plans, Policies, and Operations (PP&O).[¶] I served as a Watch Officer in the Marine Corps Operations Center (MCOC) and as the Current Operations Officer. Short touring my time in the Pentagon, I was promoted to Lieutenant Colonel and selected for Command.

Due to a number of circumstances outside of my control, I was asked to take command of a squadron I was not originally slated to command. The new squadron was HMLA-469, "Vengeance," in Camp Pendleton, a squadron of AH-1Z and UH-1Y helicopters, upgraded versions of the aircraft I flew during my first tour in the

---

* Intermediate Level School (ILS): A twelve-month resident professional military education course for Majors.

† Operations Officer (OpsO): A staff officer who plans, coordinates, and directs the training and operations for a squadron.

‡ Detachment Officer in Charge (Det OIC): The senior member of a team of Marines detached from the parent unit to conduct a deployment, mission, or training.

§ 31st Marine Expeditionary Unit (MEU): A permanently deployed Marine Air Ground Task Force (MAGTF) based in Okinawa, Japan.

¶ Plans, Policies, and Operations (PP&O): A division of Headquarters Marine Corps responsible for planning and implementing plans, policies, and concepts.

Gunfighters. Command of an HMLA was the greatest honor and the greatest challenge of my career. A squadron of over four hundred Marines and at one point thirty-one helicopters, we deployed to Okinawa, Japan, as part of the UDP. We arrived in Japan at the height of the tension between President Trump and the leader of North Korea. There would be no war, but the whole Marine Corps was on a war footing that was no longer solely focused on the Middle East.

Complete with command, I was selected to Top Level School (TLS)* at the Naval War College in Newport, Rhode Island—a huge win for me and my family, bringing us close to home one more time while on active duty. The year of school was a great time to reset my focus and motivation and spend time with my wife and son. It was also fortuitous, if I can say that about a tragic event, that we were in Newport to spend time with my parents. My father passed away while we were in Newport. It was an awful time in my life, but I was home, spending my free time with my parents, and I was able to be the first brother to get to my parents' house after receiving the news of my dad's passing. For most of my career, I would have been lucky to make it home for the funeral, never mind be the first one by Mom's side.

After school, I received orders to join the United States European Command (US EUCOM) in Stuttgart, Germany. We moved during the height of COVID-19 lockdowns. A great opportunity to live overseas and experience a Joint Tour,† serving alongside

---

* Top Level School (TLS): A twelve-month resident professional military education course for Lieutenant Colonels.

† Joint Tour: A tour of duty serving in a Joint Headquarters within the Department of Defense, providing experience across all US Military branches.

service members from each branch of the armed services. It was sometimes billed as a "Wine and Cheese Tour," which was a lie. When I joined the Future Operation Division (J35)* I found myself in an extremely difficult job surrounded by some of the best service members from across all branches of our military. I was in EUCOM for the Afghanistan Noncombatant Evacuation Operations (NEO)† and the Russian invasion of Ukraine. We made the best of our time in Germany, traveling when COVID and my work schedule would allow, but my Joint Tour was a grind I was not expecting.

Selected for promotion to Colonel, I received orders from EUCOM back to Hawaii to join Marine Forces Pacific again.

My Family

The story of my family is probably better for another book. Jennifer Haschig, now Jennifer Cherry, and I met in college. We were barely friends, but I certainly would have loved a chance to date her back then. She had a boyfriend and was off the market. I'm confident that it was better this way. I wasn't ready for her yet, and she had a lot of things she wanted to do, like becoming a doctor, before she would be willing to follow a Marine around the world.

---

* Future operations division (J35): A staff element responsible for planning and coordinating future midterm military operations, typically focusing on twenty-four to ninety-six hours beyond current operations.

† Afghanistan Noncombatant Evacuation Operations (NEO): A US-led operation to evacuate 124,000 civilians, at-risk Afghans, and Afghan citizens with special immigrant visa applications from Kabul, Afghanistan.

After I returned from a deployment to Iraq in 2006, Myspace was new. That's right: I'm *old*! I created an account and attempted to find old friends. After leaving college and becoming a Marine, I had failed to keep in touch with friends from my former life. Myspace had a function that allowed you to search for people by the school they attended. First, I searched for Bishop Feehan and then Springfield College. As I searched for Springfield College alumni, I came across a picture of Jennifer (Jenny to me). What a wonderful sight it was! And she was a chiropractor living in California—Santa Monica, to be specific. I didn't really know where Santa Monica was, but I knew it was closer to San Diego than Boston. Close enough to say hello.

I sent her a message saying something like, "Hello, remember me?" Long story short, we had a first date that turned into a dream come true. We were stuck at the hip from our first date forward, making the one hundred-plus mile trip in Southern California traffic to see each other many times a week.

We would be engaged after eight months and married within two years. There is so much more here, and I'm serious when I say it's worth another book. A book she and I can write together!

We also have Joey, our miracle baby. We tried to get pregnant for over six years with no luck and no explanation from the doctors as to why it wasn't happening. You discover when you go through this process that many more people share your sorrows, but you don't really notice, or know, until it happens to you. After many doctors' appointments, IUIs, and IVF attempts, Jenny got pregnant, and we were on the path to having Joey.

The pregnancy was a challenge for Jenny due to morning sickness. Calling it morning sickness is an understatement—for the first seven months, she had a hard time keeping any real food down. All while working and having me deployed from Hawaii to Okinawa. Other than that, the pregnancy was good, and she looked smokin' hot through the whole process.

The delivery was another story . . . He was almost two weeks late and didn't start life on his best foot. Joey, really Joseph, named after my father, was born in Castle Medical Center in Kailua, Hawaii, three days short of my birthday.

After a very long and difficult labor, when he was delivered, he was not breathing and had no heartbeat. He was revived in the room and immediately sent to Kapiolani Hospital in Honolulu, where he was put into a medically induced coma with a cooling cap that reduced the temperature of his brain to prevent the damage caused by a lack of oxygen during the delivery.

This is a very long story, but I will save the reader from wondering. He came through his first challenges with flying colors. Although the doctors told us that he would be severely disabled, unable to walk or talk or even get out of diapers, he latched on for his first feeding with Jenny when she could finally hold him. He is happy and healthy and fully abled. If you ask him, he will tell you he is a zombie because he was dead and came back to life.

The three of us have lived and traveled around the world. To the outside observer—"Instagram vs. Reality"—it may look like our life is on easy street. It is *not*. The moves, my job, Jenny starting a new chiropractic practice in each location, new friends, new schools, new homes . . . It is hard, but I wouldn't have it any other way. In fact, I think the three of us have found a way to handle this life that is also worth sharing with others.

But, as I say, that's another book. So back to this one.

The Chapters

Each chapter in this book tells a story from my career with an impactful lesson worth sharing with the world. Each chapter can be read as a stand-alone document, but the totality of the book paints a partial picture of who I am as a man and a Marine. I've organized the stories in as close to chronological order as I can, but I've purposely removed specific dates or years to disconnect events from individuals who may not want to be connected to this book.

Anyone who is named in the book is a real person who has given me permission to include them. If there is only a call sign or a billet (job title), I was unable to reach the individual or they asked me not to include them for their own reasons.

I've spent a significant amount of time reaching out to each individual to gain their permission and, more importantly, to relive the story with them. Many had vivid memories of the story and, for the most part, they aligned with my memories. Where there was a different perspective or information I didn't have, I've included that information in the chapters.

During the editing process, I shared my working draft with a few trusted people in my life. The most common critique was the difficulty of understanding some of the military concepts. In my first draft, I purposely avoided elaborating on common military- and aviation-specific concepts to shorten each chapter and focus on the lesson I want the reader to take away. It became obvious that this was a mistake.

To provide details of concepts that may be confusing to anyone outside the military or aviation, without interrupting the flow of each chapter, I've used footnotes. If you see a footnote and would like to understand a concept better, look to the bottom of each page for a detailed description of my military speak.

Like many professions, the Marine Corps has its own language, and we love our acronyms! I use them often in the book. I spell each one out after first use but not across each chapter. If you're looking for what a specific acronym is, please don't flip back in the book to find it—go straight to the Glossary of Acronyms and Terms (GOAT) at the end of the book. (And yes, I'm aware I used a new acronym to explain how I used acronyms in my book.)

Finally, the last paragraph of each chapter is also a "Readback." In these paragraphs I'm speaking to the nonmilitary reader. Here, I've summarized and rewritten each lesson in a way that anyone can pick up my book and walk away with an understanding of the lessons I strive to teach.

CHAPTER 1

Don't Fall Out

Find your motivation, even if you have to draw it from others.

I didn't know if I could keep up with the rest of the platoon in OCS. At times, I felt like my body was about to crack. The long runs, obstacle courses, and forced marches were grueling and required exceptional physical stamina. The pace of the physical activity was so demanding that I was afraid I was going to slow down just enough to "fall out."*

Falling out is something you *never* want to happen. It makes you look weak in the eyes of your instructors, your leaders. It indicates to them you might fail this period of instruction. Your peers, too, will take your falling out as a sign of weakness, as will your subordinates in the fleet. Once that happens, it may be impossible for you to effectively lead, which impacts your unit's chances of survival in combat.

* Fall out: A term typically used as a command dismissing military personnel from a formation. In this context, a person who can't maintain the pace of the formation during group physical training and begins to lag behind or stops moving altogether.

This is the reality of OCS, and surviving OCS is necessary for anyone aspiring to become an officer in the Marine Corps. Although Marines will argue that USMC basic training is the hardest, the bottom line is that any military service's basic training is difficult, and the recruits or candidates will find themselves struggling throughout the course of training.

I certainly did. There were many times when I thought I was one step away from fading down the line and out the back of a formation, even though I was in great shape.

What saved me—at the lowest point, when I thought my body couldn't keep up the pace of the rest of the team—was digging deep to find a reason to keep going. I had to find motivation within myself to take the next step. And that motivation came from an unexpected place—the other candidates. As I began to look around at the faces of the others, I realized they were all hurting too. They were all questioning the decisions they'd made to get to this place, just like me.

I'd been around OCS long enough to know who was who. When I looked around at the physical training "studs," I knew who could run three miles in under fifteen minutes; I could see that even they were not in top form. But they were still going.

I could also see that the guys who were on par with me, physically, were definitely struggling. And still going.

I looked for the candidates I knew I was faster than, the men just one step behind me in physical abilities. I looked at their faces and watched how they were running. Were they struggling? Sure they were, but they were still going, too.

In that moment, I realized: If they could do it, I could do it. If the pain in their legs was manageable, there was no reason for me to slow down either.

So I kept going.

And I never fell out.

What I discovered in OCS was that I needed to draw inspiration from those around me to keep going myself.

This lesson I learned at OCS applied to my physical fitness journey, but it applies to many other struggles as well. We may not show it on the surface, but we all struggle at different points in life, and we all need to know where we can find motivation.

When life is difficult and you don't think you can continue at its grueling pace, look around and find someone else in a similar situation. What are they doing? If they can do it, so can you. Keep pushing and never give up. Use others to inspire you if you think it's too much.

Readback

You can accomplish amazing things in life. However, accomplishing truly difficult tasks is just that—difficult! You're going to test your own internal limits and will begin to question your worth and your ability to succeed. On rare occasions, a person may be able to draw all the strength needed from within themselves, but most people will need to draw on the strength of others. You can find motivation in your personal life, from your friends, family, or coworkers. You can find motivation from celebrities in movies or on social media or from strangers on the street. When times get tough and you don't think you can keep going, look around and find the motivation you need to keep going. Don't quit. Take the next step and never give up.

CHAPTER 2

One Bite at a Time

When life gets hard, set small goals.

There are two ways to become a Marine Corps Officer: You can get an appointment to the Naval Academy, or you can attend OCS in Quantico, Virginia. OCS is the equivalent of boot camp for enlisted Marines.

I attended OCS and experienced physical and mental challenges beyond anything I'd experienced before, along with the others in my platoon. Not that I was new to overcoming challenges. Before OCS, I had played sports in high school and college, where I was stretched by the many tough challenges training and competition posed, but OCS tested me on another level. The stress imposed on the officer candidates is extreme and all-encompassing, and for a good reason: It's designed to push each candidate to the maximum stress point to see if they have what it takes to be a Marine Officer.

It all starts with the instructors. In boot camp, the enlisted staff are called Drill Instructors. At OCS, they are called Sergeant

Instructors. Two names for the same type of Marine who will push you to your limit, every day! You will never complete a task that meets or exceeds the expectations of a Sergeant Instructor. No matter how well you do, they will find something wrong with it (real or imagined) to maintain just the right amount of stress. This is not meant to break you, although it breaks some candidates; it is meant to maintain unending stress. This allows your leaders to observe your reactions—if you hold up under relentless pressure, they know you will be able to handle the far more difficult stressors of leading Marines in combat.

The tests could come at any time, often when you least expected them. For instance, I fondly remember a day in which I spent ten minutes walking into and out of a building, taking my cover (hat) on and off over and over again. It was after chow. Once a candidate finished eating, they went outside and stood by their gear until the rest of the platoon was finished. If you had to make a head call (Navy and Marine Corps speak for going to the bathroom) you were allowed to use one of the buildings next to the chow hall.

On that day, I had to make a head call. I told the candidate Platoon Sergeant where I was going—Marines must always maintain accountability—and I ran to the building that had the head we were allowed to use. As I opened the door and took off my cover to go inside, I heard a loud screeching coming from behind me. One of my Sergeant Instructors was running my way yelling at the top of his lungs, "Hello, stop, who we?"

Well, that's what I thought he was saying during my ten weeks at OCS. I figured it was just his thing and was his way of getting your attention, but I learned as we were about to graduate that he was nearly blind and needed glasses. Because Sergeant Instructors don't wear glasses, he never wore them. So, when he was asking, "Who we?" he was *really* asking who you were. It wasn't rhetorical. Funny, right?! (Had I known, I might have replied with another candidate's name . . .)

On this occasion, he'd taken my movement into the building as an opportunity to apply stress on me. I hadn't taken my cover off fast enough, so he provided me with some military education. I went in and out of the building about twenty times. Each time not moving fast enough or putting my cover on at the right time. He was inches from my face screaming at me for failing to adequately perform this basic task. At the time, I could *almost* find the humor in this situation, but I was under too much stress to really grasp it.

Now, I *love* this story. It is one of my favorites. I've told the story countless times, and it has landed well with most audiences. My best friend since second grade tells me he sometimes finds himself alone in his office saying, "Hello, stop! Who we?" and giggling about the absurdity of the story.

Why do I tell this story? To illustrate one of many challenges I faced at OCS. And to show that there was an equal amount of physical, mental, and emotional stress during those ten weeks. It was hard, and although I never thought about giving up, I was dying to find a way to mitigate the pain so I could function better and learn more during my time in Quantico, Virginia.

To get through the ten weeks, I broke things down into bite-size pieces. There were several constants each day, things that would happen no matter how good or bad your day was. You were going to eat chow three times a day, even if some were Meals, Ready-to-Eat

(MREs),* and you were going to be given the chance to sleep. Every day you could count on having chow and sleeping.

I made myself focus solely on getting to the next small step. In a single day, I went from chow to chow to chow. I could always find enough strength to get to the next chow. Once I had evening chow, I knew I was going to get into, or more accurately onto, my rack. (We only slept under our sheets on the night before we washed them—this way making our racks in the morning was faster.) And just like that, I'd made it through the day.

In the beginning of OCS, that's the goal—get through the day. You are working seven days a week and your only real break is going to church for thirty minutes on Sunday.

After the third week, candidates are allowed a day of liberty or libo (military speak for a day off) on Sunday. This isn't truly a *day* off, because you have to come back to stand duty for a four-hour block during that time, but it is *time* off! A win is a win. (And it is something recruits in boot camp don't get.)

From chow-to-chow and rack-to-rack, I expanded my focus to include "libo-to-libo." Once I had that rhythm established, the weeks seemed to pass more quickly. Before I knew it, I was halfway done and in the blink of an eye, I'd graduated from the hardest challenge of my life.

I've used the "set small goals" mentality many times in my career. On long deployments, chow-to-chow and rack-to-rack were back, though on a far less reliable schedule than at OCS!

* Meal, Ready-to-Eat (MRE): A standard military-issue packaged meal rich in calories and with a long shelf life.

During a deployment, the days took a new shape. Each day the oncoming pilots and aircrew would stage their flight gear in their assigned aircraft to ensure we were ready to take off at a moment's notice. At the same time, the off-going crews removed their gear from their assigned aircraft and ended their workday. We referred to this as standing up and standing down from the aircraft. Our crew day while deployed limited our flight window to twelve hours. After accounting for the time for briefing, standing up and standing down from the aircraft, and debriefing, a typical day lasted at least fourteen hours.

So at least I knew I would stand up and stand down from my aircraft every day. I didn't know how many or what kind of missions I would fly, but I could count on my day ending at some point, so I focused on that.

As a longer-range goal, I added the times I would get to talk to my wife (or fiancée, depending on the deployment) once or twice a week. I looked forward to the next conversation so much, even though, back in the olden days, before Wi-Fi—I know, I know, this was in the early 2000s—to talk to your family you had to wait in line to use a landline phone that would often have a three- to five-second delay.

It was difficult on both ends, but just hearing your loved one's voice paid huge dividends. Even if Jenny didn't always know what to say. She would keep Post-it notes to remember all the things she wanted to tell me, but she would still spend eight minutes of the ten we had talking about how funny the most recent episode of *The Office* was.

On my deployments I was chow-to-chow, stand up-to-stand down, rack-to-rack, and Jenny-to-Jenny. I had my small steps to get through each day and week and before I knew it, seven months had gone by and I was on my way home.

Readback

You don't have to go to OCS or combat to have a hard time seeing an end to your daily struggles. We all face big challenges in life. Some of us struggle every day with depression or grief from the loss of a loved one or the loss of an opportunity to get to the next level in life. Others battle anxiety or a mental illness that obscures their view of the world beyond their difficulties.

However, even amid the hardships of life, we can all break our daily and weekly lives down into small pieces that we know we can accomplish, at an interval we can manage. Some days that might be minute-to-minute, which is a fine place to start.

As my mother-in-law loves to say, "How do you eat an elephant? One bite at a time!"

She might be on to something.

So try it out. Take each challenge one small piece at a time. If you do this well, you will see that you are better at managing your daily challenges than you originally thought and you can start to extend the time intervals. Once you begin to manage the small steps with ease, you get stronger and can extend the time intervals for each small goal into something more significant.

CHAPTER 3

Forever in Their Debt

Never underestimate small acts of kindness.

There's a healthy rivalry between HMLA Squadrons in the Marine Corps. The same is also true for West Coast and East Coast squadrons, and between the squadrons on the flight line at both Marine Corps Air Station Camp Pendleton and Marine Corps Air Station New River.

I had a bias for my first Fleet squadron, the HMLA-369 "Gunfighters," after my first interaction with my on wing* in flight school, which I cover in a later chapter. He was the first to explain the competition between Camp Pendleton–based squadrons and the rivalry between the Gunfighters and the HMLA-169 "Vipers."

The Vipers had a unique culture summarized by their slogan: "We hate each other but we hate you more!" They wore this as a

* On Wing: A Student Naval Aviator is assigned a specific instructor during the initial phase of flight school. The pairing allows instructors to closely monitor development and progress through critical periods of instruction.

badge of honor, and it showed in the way they interacted with other squadrons. While I was a Gunfighter, we began to respond to any mention of the Vipers by simulating spitting on the ground. You couldn't say the word Vipers without someone in the room making a spitting sound.

Now, with all this rivalry bullshit aside, the Vipers (*hack spit*) were an excellent squadron of professional officers. Some of my favorite Cobra and Huey pilots were junior officers, or "boots,"* in the Vipers while I was a boot in the Gunfighters. In 2003, during the first days and weeks of Operation Iraqi Freedom (OIF), the Viper copilots were some of the most heroic pilots of the war. They were overhead the Marines as they pushed from Kuwait to Baghdad. They saved and they took countless lives, and the ground forces didn't want to move without HMLA pilots overhead. Their aircraft were shot full of holes and many of them were shot down; a few were shot down multiple times.

I was in Marine Helicopter Training Squadron 303 (HMT-303),† the Cobra and Huey training squadron, when OIF started. I graduated from HMT-303 just after the Marines reached Baghdad and there was an attempt to get as many pilots into the war as possible—we didn't know this war would last for more than twenty years. First Lieutenant "Sponge" Haines, First Lieutenant "Goose" Topper, and I were given five days' notice to pack our shit and get

---

* Boot: A term derived from "Boot Camp" is typically used to describe new Marines. It's often used in a disparaging way, but it can also be used affectionately.

† Marine Helicopter Training Squadron 303 (HMT-303): Now called Marine Light Attack Helicopter Training Squadron-303 (HMLAT-303) conducts initial and refresher training for pilots and aircrew of UH-1 and AH-1 helicopters.

on a plane to Kuwait and join the Gunfighters. The squadron was already deployed in support of OIF alongside the Vipers.

Joining an HMLA as a boot is difficult, but joining an HMLA deployed to combat as a boot is terrifying. My first flight in a fleet squadron was at the start of a five-day mission from Kuwait into Iraq. My first flight during low-light-level, moonless nighttime conditions on Night Vision Goggles (NVGs) was on the border of Iraq and Iran.

I was as green as any pilot could be and I was in combat.

As soon as my first five-day mission into Iraq was complete, the Gunfighters were given orders to return to Camp Pendleton to reset and deploy to Okinawa, Japan, as part of the continuation of the UDP. The Marine Aircraft Group 39 (MAG-39)* Commander wanted to maximize the combat flying experience of his pilots. This meant that Sponge and I were ordered to fly with the Vipers for one more multiday mission into Iraq. We spent five more days flying in Iraq and returned to Kuwait just in time to join back up with the Gunfighters on their movement back to the United States.

Because the Gunfighters were redeploying back to Southern California, they had begun taking steps to return home, such as destroying—burning—the maps the squadron created for missions in Iraq. These, it turned out, were maps I would need for my missions with the Vipers. (At the time, all the maps were updated by hand to show the airspace coordination measures used in support of combat operations. Because I joined the Gunfighters late, I didn't make my own.)

---

* Marine Aircraft Group 39 (MAG-39): A Camp Pendleton–based unit currently consisting of multiple AH-1Z, UH-1Y, and MV-22 aircraft and an aviation logistics squadron.

Reality started to sink in. The Gunfighter maps had been destroyed and the Viper copilots needed theirs for future missions. I had no time to make new maps—that would have taken days of dedicated work.

Then, without being asked, First Lieutenant Matt "Dog Nuts" Daigneault offered me his. This may sound like a small offering of little consequence, but, to me—an ill-prepared, brand-new HMLA pilot forced to fly with another squadron in combat—it was a gift from God.

Dog Nuts didn't have to do this for me. We knew each other but not so well that I would expect him to go out of his way to help me. He offered them freely and with good humor. I think he saw the situation I was in and had pity on me.

I'll never forget this act of kindness. I can see us in the one-hundred-degree-plus heat under a cloudless sky, standing next to a green Quadcon and him opening his maps for me to see. He was a larger-than-life Marine with a very deep voice and a unique sense of humor. That day, he removed a large, if figurative, rock from my pack and made my quick transition across to the Vipers a success. I haven't seen or talked to him in years, but I am forever in his debt. There is nothing I wouldn't do to help him in a time of need.

The other Viper who showed me kindness was First Lieutenant Dale "Amish" Behm. He was the copilot of the Dash-2 aircraft, or wingman, in the Viper section I was scheduled to fly with. He had already had several harrowing flights and would have a few more before his days of combat operations were complete.

I was scheduled to fly with a talented, no-nonsense WTI Captain with encyclopedic knowledge of just about anything in an HMLA. He was on his second combat deployment—his first was part of a MEU Aviation Combat Element (MEU ACE)* that went ashore at the start of the Afghanistan war—and he was laser focused on accomplishing the mission and keeping his squadron mates alive. He wasn't happy to be flying with me and didn't make it a secret, but I managed not to back down from his frustration and anger and in the long run I earned his respect. Not that we were friendly—during my time as his combat crew,† we didn't speak unless it was directly related to planning or flying our missions.

Amish is a smart man, and he could see the dynamic created by my arrival in the Vipers. He went out of his way to pull me aside and help me to navigate the interpersonal challenges I was having in my cockpit and to become a better functioning combat crew. He gave me pointers, talking me through procedures and explaining what would be expected of me before and during missions. He could have sat back and watched the train wreck, but he didn't. He took time out of his day, multiple times a day, to help me. It wasn't his job, and I wasn't a Viper, but he helped me. I will forever be in his debt as well. His small acts of kindness helped me through this challenging time and made me a more capable combat crew.

In both cases, they were just being themselves, consummate professionals, great Marines, and even better men. I don't know if they saw their kindness as anything more than being their true selves. However, their small acts of kindness were life-changing for

---

* Marine Expeditionary Unit Aviation Combat Element (MEU ACE): The MEU's ACE provides the airpower including transport, attack, and support aircraft, ensuring the MEU can effectively operate over long ranges in diverse environments.

† Combat Crew: While deployed in support of combat operations, an HMLA squadron typically pairs pilots and aircrew together for weeks or months to improve crew coordination and increase mission effectiveness.

me. Each of them single-handedly changed my situation and made me better. I've carried these lessons with me for my whole career. I will carry them with me for the rest of my life.

Readback

Never underestimate the effect an act of kindness can have on someone. What may be perceived as insignificant for the giver can be life-changing for the recipient. Don't miss an opportunity to freely, with no expectation of reciprocation, help someone in need. A few minutes of your time can change the life of someone else. You may be fortunate enough to see the positive results but, in most cases, you will never know the long-lasting effect of your actions. Never miss an opportunity to be kind and to lend a helping hand to someone in need.

CHAPTER 4

Are You Working Hard Enough?

Break out of the pack.

After my short deployment to Iraq in 2003, HMLA-369 had a brief dwell period at our home station aboard Camp Pendleton before deploying again, this time to Okinawa, Japan, as part of the Marine Corps' UDP, a long-standing continuous rotational deployment of select Marine Corps units from the United States to Japan.

I found this frustrating, and so did many in our squadron. There was a feeling that our time and talent was being wasted in Japan. We could have been refitting in California, preparing for our next deployment to Iraq! (Had I known how many times I was going to have to go to Iraq, my attitude might have been different.)

At the time, I lacked an understanding of the operational and strategic importance of deploying to Japan. I was eager to get plenty of "red time," a term used for entries in our aviation logbooks denoting flight time in support of combat operations, which were written in red ink.

There was a lot I didn't appreciate about being there at first, but I would come to see it differently over time. During this eight-month deployment, we had the opportunity to conduct exercises in South Korea, the Philippines, and Thailand. And I was surrounded by some of the best friends I would ever make and a group of instructors who would shape my career as a Cobra pilot. Looking back, it was an amazing time in my life.

However, at the time I was frustrated. I had graduated in the top 1 percent of all flight school graduates, gotten my first choice of airframe, flown my first fleet hours in a Cobra in combat, and was slightly deflated to be missing an opportunity to return to combat. I hadn't taken my foot off the gas, but I had more to give.

My peer group was very strong. Some had been with the squadron for the deployment to Iraq and a few others joined the Gunfighters prior to deploying to Japan. We were talented and dedicated. Of the eight Cobra pilots who stayed in the Marine Corps until retirement, all would become NSIs, five would become WTIs, five would become Commanding Officers, three would become Colonels, and if they had stayed in past Lieutenant Colonel, I'm convinced two would have become General Officers.

This was great for the squadron, but it posed a problem for the instructors whose job it was to train us: They had an accomplished group before them and only so many options for moving people up.

Ironically, by doing well and progressing in a pack, we were limiting our individual opportunities to achieve high-level qualifications and designations.* It's just math: Because there are a finite number of flight hours, the operations department can only progress so many pilots at a time. They hope to ultimately progress everyone who is capable, but there are no guarantees. To pick a few pilots to accelerate to meet the squadron's training requirements, they must rank the peer group and bet on the best, first.

We were tight and we were keeping pace with each other, always working together, and understanding how lucky we were to be in such great company. In my career I saw peer groups like ours and I saw peer groups who, almost to a person, were weak, producing only one or two quality officers. We didn't have that problem; we were strong, and the squadron could see it.

I didn't anticipate the logjam that was coming, and at some point in time I lost the edge I had in flight school to be first to select Cobras. Had I lost my drive? I don't think so . . . But as I reflect on where I was at the time, I can see that I wasn't sure how long I'd stay in the Marine Corps, whether I was going to make it a career or get out after my first obligation was up. I was also battling the voice in my head, the one asking me if I was good enough to become an NSI or WTI.

Fortunately, one of the Iron Captains in the squadron, Captain "MOG" Marvel, could see through the fog and was willing to act. I can still remember the day he brought one of my best friends and me into his Bachelor Officer Quarters room to talk to us about what our goals were for our time in the squadron.

---

* Qualifications and Designations: Achieved levels of excellence and proficiency in core skills and flight leadership within a squadron's mission-essential task.

I had never been in his room; we were not friends at this time, and First Lieutenants didn't just wander into the Captain's rooms.* I knew he was smart, direct, angry, and he talked fast. And that he often had skin peeling from his forehead and a bit of a twisted sense of humor. MOG was senior in rank and experience but he had a polarizing personality, like many HMLA pilots.

MOG made our situation clear: We needed to break out of the pack. We were all doing well, but the thinning of the herd was coming. If we wanted to make the cut, we had to start demonstrating how we were better than our peers and the peer groups ahead of us, and why we should be the one to lead the squadron when we returned from this deployment. We needed to outshine them in planning, studying, briefing, and flying. This resonated with me but not as much as it could have.

We did break out of the pack, and I did try harder after that session with our unlikely mentor. I was able to surpass many pilots in the peer group ahead of me, and no one from the peer group behind me was able to surpass me. But my peer group was strong, and there were a few who would be difficult to beat out for the first few NSI and WTI opportunities! Of this peer group of fifteen pilots,

---

* The gradient between a First Lieutenant and a Captain in an HMLA is immense. In other aviation communities, Captains and First Lieutenants are grouped up as part of the Junior Officer Protection Association (JOPA). The JOPA teams up against the senior (field grade) officers to provide collective defense. An HMLA is *not* this way. A First Lieutenant is a *boot* and a boot is a boot. Junior officers in an HMLA are copilots. On most combat missions the copilot is in the front seat of the Cobra, acting as the gunner. Most shooting from a Cobra happens in the front seat. If you are not a professional who can be trusted, your action or inaction can and will result in the death of the wrong people. To those not in the military, I'm sure this sounds crazy. In an HMLA, it is our way of life.

when it came down to those who would become AH-1W WTIs, I would fall out at number four of six that would make it to Marine Aviation Weapons and Tactics Squadron-1 (MAWTS-1)* and become a WTI.

You may think I'm upset about this fact . . . I'll admit that part of me is disappointed that I didn't get the nod earlier, but I'm also honored to have made the cut at all. Most don't go to WTI. I'm also clear-eyed about the fact that the three picked ahead of me were outstanding Marines. "Fredo" Federico, "Ponch" Robb, and "IRA" Clarke deserved their places in the pecking order. Two of them would have been General Officers had they stayed in past Lieutenant Colonel.

The bottom line is I tried hard—harder than I might have if I hadn't been in the company of such accomplished peers—and I did break out of the pack. But I don't know what else I could have done to beat those three out; they were that good. And I was lucky to stand alongside them. They made me better as a Marine, a pilot, a friend, and a person. Each one of them stood beside me as a groomsman at my wedding.

---

* Marine Aviation Weapons and Tactics Squadron-1 (MAWTS-1): The Marine Corps premier training squadron responsible for hosting two seven-week training courses for prospective Weapons and Tactics Instructors (WTIs) and providing standardized advanced and tactical training and certification of unit instructor qualifications to support Marine aviation training and readiness.

Readback

If you want to succeed in life, there may be times when you are working hard but you need to work even harder to break out of the pack. If you want to do great things or be great, look around. Who else is as good as you are, or better? Find them and self-assess. Are they better, or are you not working hard enough? Don't lose an opportunity because you think you're giving it your all. If you are and you're outdone by someone else, fine. But you better know it before you let it pass you by.

CHAPTER 5

"I Can't Turn Left"

You may be surprised by who saves the day.

In the military, especially in aviation, you might convince yourself that only the most senior or experienced pilots or crew chiefs will return from a difficult mission as the hero. This may often be the case, but they are not the only heroes around. Never allow yourself to lose sight of the talent of everyone else around you. In an HMLA, we fly multi-piloted and crewed aircraft.* When things get difficult, the whole crew relies on each other to accomplish the mission and come home safely, and you may be surprised by who saves the day.

While deployed to Iraq in 2007, I was preparing to attend the MAWTS-1, WTI Course. I already had all the training prerequisites to attend the course, but to maximize the number of additional

* Multi-pilot and crewed aircraft: An AH-1W Cobra has two pilots with one typically flying from the back seat while the other acts as a gunner from the front seat. In a UH-1N, two pilots sit side-by-side and two crew chiefs man weapons from doors on either side of the aircraft cabin.

qualifications and designations I could obtain *during* the course, there were a few training events I could complete at the squadron before going to WTI.

One of the prerequisites the squadron wanted me to have before I left Iraq for WTI was the first of two training events in the Forward Air Control (Airborne) Instructor (FAC(A)I) syllabus.* This designation allows WTIs to instruct other pilots how to provide terminal control of aircraft,† fixed-wing and rotary-wing, during Close Air Support (CAS)‡ missions in support of Marines on the ground. The FAC(A)I designation is extremely difficult to do; it requires complete mastery of your aircraft and knowledge of other CAS aircraft capabilities, crew coordination within your aircraft and other aircraft in your flight, understanding of the ground scheme of maneuver, and the geometry required to deliver lethal fires while protecting friendly forces and innocent civilians. This designation is also difficult to achieve for several training and programmatic reasons I won't go into in this book.

At this time, back-to-back deployments to Iraq had driven the aviation community to seek opportunities to progress its pilots

---

* Forward Air Controller (Airborne) Instructor (FAC(A)I): An instructor who can teach other pilots to control aircraft while conducting attacks in support of ground units from the pilot's seat of their aircraft.

† Terminal Control: Real-time direction and clearance of aircraft ordnance delivered during Close Air Support (CAS) missions. Performed by certified Forward Air Controllers (FAC), Forward Air Controllers-Airborne (FAC-A), or Joint Tactical Air Controllers (JTAC), it ensures precision, coordination with maneuvering ground forces, and the safe and effective execution of airstrikes in close proximity to friendly forces.

‡ Close Air Support (CAS): Air-to-ground attacks against hostile targets in close proximity to friendly forces requiring detailed integration of each attack between the pilots and a Forward Air Controller (FAC) or Joint Terminal Attack Controller.

while deployed in combat. In 2003, this never would have happened—in fact, the idea would have been laughed at—but after four years of continuous rotations to Iraq, more ranges were identified to allow pilots to progress on a case-by-case basis.

A range was established approximately forty miles west of Al Asad Airbase in the Al Anbar Province of Iraq. It was well away from any populated areas, allowing for training similar to what we could accomplish in the ranges back home.

To maximize my opportunity to get my FAC(A)I designation during the WTI course, I needed to complete the first event at night with a section of F/A-18s and a section of attack or utility helicopters (skids). The total requirement was six aircraft: 1x AH-1W and 1x UH-1N in my section, 1x AH-1W and 1x UH-1N section from an East Coast HMLA based out of Al Asad, and a section of 2x F/A-18s based out of Al Asad. These aircraft, operating as three separate elements, were needed for me to demonstrate the ability to *safely* and effectively control multiple CAS elements in close proximity to (simulated) friendly ground forces attacking an enemy position.

The mission started off well with clear skies and light winds under a quarter moon. I was flying from the back seat and my instructor pilot for the day was one of my best friends, Captain Jeffrey "Ponch" Robb. While instructing me from the front seat, he was playing the part of a student getting his first night FAC(A) syllabus event. Forcing me to lead the flight, fly the aircraft, and provide oversight, instruction, and quality assurance over his action in the cockpit while controlling the two other sections conducting CAS.

Captain Ryan "Moby" Jacobs and Captain Andy "Francis" Graham were the pilots of our Dash-2 aircraft. Moby was the squadron's UH-1N WTI and Francis was another up-and-coming copilot. He was the junior pilot in the flight but, like me, he was preparing for WTI. He needed to complete one last training event to meet the requirements to attend the course. The two crew chiefs in the back of the UH-1N were Corporal Mike Defeo and Lance Corporal Bart Davis.

All players were on station and the flight was going well. My section had anchored on the only piece of terrain on the range, a small crescent-shaped hill in the middle of a flat desert that we called Rotary Wing Hill. With the exception of the attack runs we made, we spent the majority of the mission holding in a right turn over the small hilltop at three hundred to five hundred feet.

Because Francis needed to complete his training to attend WTI, Ponch and I passed lead to Moby to ensure Francis completed his event first. Once they met their requirements, the lead was passed back to us, and I took control of the aircraft and the mission.

As the mission progressed the wind began to increase. When we arrived on station, the winds were at ten knots from the northwest. After the first few attacks, the wind continued to increase and the visibility in the objective area began to decrease. With twenty minutes left on station, the wind increased to thirty knots and the visibility dropped to less than three miles. We directed the other section of skids to return to base and continued giving 9-line* attack briefs to the F/A-18s.

After a few more minutes, the wind increased to over forty knots and the visibility began rapidly reducing. With ten minutes left on

* 9-Lines: Nine standardized lines of information given to an attacking aircraft during Close Air Support missions. The type of information in each line is standardized, allowing the ground controller and pilots to quickly and safely bring lethal fires against an enemy position.

station, we terminated training and sent the jets home. With my training successfully completed, all I had to do was get our section back to Al Asad for gas. This should have been easy. It wasn't.

By the time we were ready to turn toward Al Asad, the visibility had dropped to between a quarter and an eighth of a mile and the wind was steady at forty knots.* At this point, we could look down and see the ground and about six hundred feet ahead of the aircraft—it felt like we were flying inside a green-tinted snow globe filled with fine, floating sand. Not good! To compound the problem, I had been holding—flying a predictable racetrack pattern around a known point—in a right turn for about thirty minutes. On what should have been my last lap in holding, I inadvertently slowed the aircraft to forty knots as I turned into the wind—the forty-knot wind. The aircraft was technically still in forward flight. I looked down at the ground three hundred feet below.

We were not moving. This was the beginning of the end for me. Clearly on the edge of full-blown vertigo,† I pushed the nose over and pulled in collective‡ for more power to pick up airspeed as I continued my right turn with the intention of rolling out on a heading of 090 (east) toward Al Asad. As the 090 heading came and

---

* Weather minimums: Visibility and cloud clearance requirements to conduct an instrument approach into an airport are typically higher than this, especially for helicopters without integrated precision approach equipment.

† Vertigo: A false sense of motion pilots can experience during bad weather, high workloads, or with excessive movement of the head. Vertigo can lead to disorientation and incapacitation and is often a causal factor in aviation mishaps.

‡ Helicopter collective: A primary flight control lever used to control the aircraft's vertical lift through a mechanical link to change the pitch of the rotor blades while simultaneously directing the engines to add or reduce power output.

went, Ponch asked me what I was doing. I told him I was doing one last lap in holding and I would turn toward Al Asad. On the next pass, I blew right through the heading again and Ponch said, "What are you doing? Roll out 090!"

In the aviation world, there is a term called the "Hand of God." It is used to describe a phenomenon where you know what you are supposed to do with your hands on the flight controls, but there is an invisible force preventing you from moving the controls in the proper direction. It's like God has placed his hand on yours and will not allow you to move the controls. Sounds crazy, right? Well, it's real and God's hand touched me that night.

This was my *Zoolander* moment.* I told Ponch, "I can't turn left!"

He said, "What do you mean you can't turn left?!"

My immediate response was, "I can't fucking turn left. I have vertigo!"

Ponch quickly took the controls and began what should have been our last lap in holding. Once again, we approached our roll out heading of 090 and he blew right past it, continuing the turn in our holding pattern.

Now it was my turn to be worried. As we passed through 090, I asked why he didn't roll out and he said, "I can't turn left either, I have vertigo!" We were officially "assholes and elbows" in the cockpit. Between the two of us we had well over three thousand hours of flight time, we'd just completed one of the most difficult training events we have in our syllabus, each of us was on our third combat deployment, and we could not turn toward home.

---

* *Zoolander* moment: A reference to the popular movie *Zoolander* where the lead character Derek, a male model, describes his inability to "turn left."

I took the controls back from him and we began working through our options. One option was to land at the base of Rotary Wing Hill on the range. That bad idea quickly fell off the list of viable options when a previously unknown set of headlights came on at the base of the hilltop. There were no friendlies in the area, and we weren't going to find out if the non-friendly headlights were enemy or not. To this day, I don't know who was in the vehicle and what would have happened had we decided to land.

Still in holding, we began communicating our problems to Moby and his crew. We fessed up that we both had vertigo and asked if they could take the lead and bring us home. What Ponch and I didn't know at the time was that in their cockpit, Moby immediately said "nope" and both crew chiefs had vertigo too. But Francis, the most junior pilot in the flight, didn't hesitate for a moment.

At three hundred feet above the ground in an eighth of a mile visibility, Francis took the controls, flipped his goggles up, and transitioned to an instrument scan. Their aircraft turned inside ours, rolling out on 090 this time (no more holding) and began to lead us home. I was still flying, and I slowly closed in on their aircraft, tucked into as close to a parade position* as I could, and held on for dear life.

With Francis flying, Moby retained communications with external agencies. As we got close to ten miles from Al Asad, we heard our F/A-18s conduct a missed approach because the weather

---

* Parade position: A non-tactical formation where the wingman joins in close proximity to the lead aircraft. This formation is typically seen during air shows but is useful while operating in congested airspace and during poor weather conditions.

was too low for them to safely land at the airfield. This removed the option for us to climb to altitude and shoot an approach,* and we didn't have enough gas to get to an alternate. We were committed to our low-level approach to landing.

Once in contact with the tower, they told us to hold outside of ten miles. Moby explained to them that we would not be holding and that we were inbound for landing with no delay. After multiple polite transmissions with the tower controllers, he stopped asking and started telling them what we were doing.

We landed safely, and then the shaking started. Although this was only a training mission, we were all completely fried. I sat in the aircraft for a long time after shutting down because I wasn't sure my legs were going to work. Once out of the aircraft, I literally bent down and kissed the ground, and then we all found each other and hugged the way Maverick and Iceman did at the end of *Top Gun*.

With zero hesitation, the most junior pilot in our crew had stepped up to the challenge and brought us home safely. Francis was the hero that day, and I will never forget his actions or the lesson that teamwork matters. Never underestimate the power of the team and, in this case, the heroic efforts even the most junior member of your team can muster.

---

* Shoot an approach: A term used when an aircraft flies an instrument approach to an airport, typically during reduced visibility caused by low clouds or, in this case, dust storms.

Readback

Never underestimate the talent of those who work around you. You may be the smartest and most talented person in the room. You may have the most experience and be *the* expert in your field. However, your expertise doesn't remove the talent, initiative, and skills of those who work with and for you. There will come a time when you don't have the answer or the ability to accomplish a task. Start looking into the talents of your team now to understand their strengths and weaknesses. Don't wait until you "can't turn left." Draw on those talents now and allow them to grow in your organization. You won't always use their ideas or approach, but you will understand them better and know where to go when you begin to reenact your own personal *Zoolander* scene.

CHAPTER 6

Are You the Weak Link?

Don't be the FARP planner.

In the last chapter, I talked about how the most junior member of your team might surprise you and be the one to save the day. That's true. On the other hand, there may be times when you are the "weak link"—the one who is unaware that they can't be trusted.

In the military, at least as a Cobra pilot, you learn to spot the weakest link very fast. When you walk into a room of Marines tasked with accomplishing a difficult problem, you quickly figure out who is in charge and who is the weakest link. Now, to be fair, the weakest link may be a talented individual who is just slightly less talented than the next person. Or, the weakest link may be well behind their peers, but not realize it—often, they are oblivious to where they stand in the group.

Honestly, you might not have to look as far as you think. The next time you're in a room full of people working on a difficult task, take a step back and look around. If you can't find the weakest link, you might be in trouble. It's probably you! Maybe you're not good at your job or maybe you can't be trusted to accomplish difficult tasks without direct and constant supervision.

So how can you tell who is the weakest link, and if you're it?

Imagine you're a student at the MAWTS-1. It is the premier school for Marine Corps aviation, a six-week course packed with classes, tests, dynamic planning, and some of the most challenging and, in many cases, fun flying you will ever do. The school produces WTIs who are charged with developing and running the training plans for their squadrons. All WTI graduates get a unique shoulder patch, sometimes called the "chicken patch,"* to designate them as Subject Matter Experts in Marine aviation.

Every flight is preceded by an intense planning evolution designed to test the students' analytical and planning skills. Students have a compressed window for planning—hours, not days—to develop a plan and a brief to accomplish their mission. The WTI class progresses in phases of increasing complexity, starting small with missions designed for your specific airframe and growing to fully coordinated missions integrating all functions of Marine Aviation† with the Ground Combat Elements (GCE)‡ scheme of maneuver.

---

* The "Chicken Patch": A shoulder patch with the head of a bald eagle, designating you as a WTI and a leader in your squadron. It gives you instant credibility when you walk into a room of aviators.

† Functions of Marine Aviation: The Marine Corps has six primary functions: assault support, anti-air warfare, offensive air support, electronic warfare, control of aircraft and missile, and aerial reconnaissance.

‡ Ground Combat Element (GCE): The land forces, primarily consisting of Infantry units, of the Marine Air-Ground Task Force (MAGTF). The other two components of the MAGTF are the Aviation Combat Element (ACE) and Logistics Combat Element (LCE).

During each planning event, students must account for all aspects of the mission, from the most complex and high-speed elements to the most basic and mundane tasks. All are important and even the mundane tasks can be mission critical. One example of a mundane but critical task is planning for the Forward Arming and Refueling Point (FARP).* If the FARP isn't planned properly, the mission is a failure because the aircraft don't have enough fuel to accomplish the desired end state.

FARP planning is the bread and butter of a planning evolution. It takes time and coordination across mission partners, but there are standard planning numbers and safety measures across the fleet. It isn't a dynamic task requiring direct supervision by the lead planners.

Don't get me wrong; I'm not saying that anyone who's tasked with developing the FARP diagram is the weakest link. Far from it. I am saying if you're at MAWTS-1 as a prospective WTI student and your peers will only allow you to plan for the FARP, you are the weakest link.

Step one in correcting this problem is realizing that your peers don't trust you, or at a minimum, they trust you the least. Be self-aware. Step two is fixing the problem. It will be difficult to change their perception of you in the middle of a planning evolution. But you can improve over time. Up your game in everything you do. Show up to planning events, even when you're not flying. Start helping others when your efforts benefit them but have no effect on you. When the pressure to perform in planning and in flight is reduced, it will be easier to learn from others. Show some

* Forward Arming and Refueling Point (FARP): A mobile location capable of providing rotary-wing and fixed-wing aircraft with fuel and ordnance.

"give a shit" and take advantage of opportunities to focus on tasks more dynamic than the FARP diagram.

Readback

If you're someone who is happy with being "the FARP planner," this book probably isn't for you. For the rest, I hope a light bulb just came on over your head. The real world is not as black and white as a military planning evolution, but there is a pecking order in all aspects of our life. Take a step back and see where you stand in your personal and professional circles. Are you relegated to the most menial of tasks? If you are and that's okay, there is nothing wrong with you. If you are and that's not okay, act now. It may be uncomfortable at first, but work every day to be a better employee or teammate. Become brilliant at the basics and earn the trust of those around you. Volunteer for more challenging tasks and give your full effort to provide the best possible results. Become a team player and an expert at your task, and you will earn or rebuild the trust within your organization.

CHAPTER 7

Fight for What's Right

Speak truth to power.

I joined the Marine Corps to become an AH-1W Cobra pilot. I wanted to be a Marine and I wanted to fly Cobras. Period.

This sentiment is rare in flight school. Most Student Naval Aviators (SNAs)* want to fly jets. When it comes time to choose between jets, helicopters, and transports, most SNAs who are not eligible for jets are disheartened. Jets are the prized goal.

Students work toward this goal beginning with the initial phase in flight school, called Primary. During Primary, every event is graded. Each written test, brief, and flight is graded, resulting in a standardized score called a Navy Standard Score (NSS). To continue in flight training after Primary, the student must attain a minimum NSS score. If you want to be eligible for selection for jets,

* Student Naval Aviator (SNA): Term used for service members from the Navy and Marine Corps while training in flight school.

you have to achieve a different—much higher—minimum NSS score, referred to as "jet grades."

In most cases, anyone with jet grades selects jets if staffing goals allow. But not me. My dad was a crew chief in helicopters, and I'd had a fascination with Cobras and Hueys for my whole life. I wanted to be like my father in more ways than I can capture in this book. One of those ways was to be a helicopter pilot, *not* a jet pilot.

The rarity of my mentality was highlighted when I met my "on wing" in VT-3, the Red Knights. All of a student's initial flights are with the same person, referred to as their "on wing." This arrangement ensures you receive the same input and techniques to build a habit pattern without having to adjust to many different instructional techniques. It helps you learn faster.

In the first meeting with my on wing, Major Mark "Naugy" Warner asked me what I wanted to fly. I answered, "Cobras," and he told me to stop being a kiss ass. Confused, I asked him what he meant. He was a Cobra pilot, a fact that I was unaware of, and he thought I was sucking up to him. I explained to him that I was serious and gave him my reasons why. Seemingly happy with my response, he told me I better be a Gunfighter!

Because I was a Marine or because he was a Marine or because I wanted to be a Cobra pilot, Major Warner was demanding of me as an on wing. He held me to very high standards and corrected me on any small deviation. My grades with him were just average, which humbled me and made me question if I was good enough to be in flight school.

But on my first off wing flight, I realized just how high Major Warner's standards were. The other instructors were not the same. A small deviation from altitude in the traffic pattern, a slight delay in a radio call or recall of an emergency procedure, anything that would have resulted in average grade on a flight with Major Warner suddenly translated to an above-average performance. Apparently, I was far better at flying than I'd thought. It was still difficult, requiring a lot of hard work, but my scores went through the roof. His strictness with me built habit patterns that many of my peers didn't have. My own expectations of performance in all phases of flight school were higher than that of my off wing instructors. I had higher expectations for myself than they did.

By the end of the Primary phase, I had jet grades. A huge accomplishment for anyone and I was very proud.

But then came the moment of truth: Upon completion of Primary, you are required to provide a wish list, ranking your preferences in priority order: helicopters, jets, or transports. I filled out my card in that order, unaware of what was coming my way.

I was on base at the Navy Exchange, awaiting news of who got what, when a person I barely knew told me the Training Wing Commanding Officer* was looking for me. I had never met him and didn't know much about the Command structure of flight school past my instructor for the day . . . I immediately stopped what I was doing and headed to the Training Wing headquarters.

While walking from the parking lot to the building, I was stopped by another student pilot who told me the CO was looking for me. Very strange . . . I started trying to remember what I had done last weekend. Was I in trouble!?!

---

* Training Wing Commanding Officer: A Navy Captain or Marine Colonel in command of a wing of flight school training squadrons.

As I entered the Command Deck and the CO's secretary saw me, she picked up the phone and said, "He's here." My heart stopped; I thought I was in a lot of trouble.

I walked into his office and reported to him. He told me to sit down and after a short time, he got to the point. He wanted to know why I didn't want to fly jets and explained to me how the Marine Corps needed jet pilots. He told me my Primary grades indicated I would succeed as a jet pilot.

I explained to him why I joined the Marine Corps and what I wanted to fly. He continued to sell me on the benefit of flying jets, telling me how Cobras are tactical, just like jets. I knew that my wish list was just that, a wish, and that he had the authority to tell me what platform I would be selected for. This conversation could have been one-way and over very quickly. As it was, we had some back-and-forth, and finally, I was backed into a corner. I had to make my last attempt to get what I had worked for and what I thought was right.

I told him I had jet grades for the simple reason that I gave my best during every training event. I told him I knew I could have "gamed the game" by being an average performer guaranteed to be selected for the helicopter pipeline. But I did not. I told him I was really hoping that I wouldn't be punished for doing my best when something less could have resulted in what I really wanted.

He did not expect that response from me. At first, I thought he was upset. As I sat there in his office, frozen in place, realizing what I had just said, I could feel the foundation of my young career shaking under my feet. After what felt like an hour, he responded to me. He told me he would allow me to put rotary wing, and only rotary wing, on my wish list. And that I "better get fucking Cobras!"

This moment was pivotal to me, in my life and my career. It gave me my first glimpse into who I would become as a Marine and a Cobra pilot. At this point, I didn't know Boyd's concept of "to be or to do." This concept defines your choices when you come to a fork in the road that can have significant consequence. If you choose "to be," you do what you're told but may have to come to terms with a moral dilemma. If you choose "to do," you fight for what you think is best, or right, at the risk of ending your career. (You will learn more about Boyd in a later chapter.)

I also didn't know who I was to become as a Marine and a person. There was an angry Captain living inside me; I just hadn't met him yet. I would grow into him and mature past him, always knowing he was there (whether to help or hinder wasn't always clear).

This is the first real example of me speaking truth to power. I didn't plan it, but I felt the need to fight for what I thought was right; that need was ingrained in me, even as a Second Lieutenant in flight school.

Of course, the conversation could have gone the other way. It could have left me crippled in flight school. That CO could have made my life extremely difficult. To his credit, the next and only other time I saw him was the day I officially became a pilot. At my "Winging,"* he came up to me and congratulated me on getting Cobras.

I don't know if it was luck, his character, my delivery, or a combination of all three, but he heard me and allowed me to have control over my future in the Marine Corps.

---

* Winging: A traditional ceremony where flight school students graduate and become Naval Aviators.

The Gunfighters

After completing my training to become a Cobra Pilot at HMT-303, I joined my first fleet squadron, HMLA-369, the "Gunfighters." I joined the squadron as a First Lieutenant and departed as a Captain.

Most people spend three to four years in a squadron before taking orders to a B-Billet, a job outside of your MOS. A B-Billet could be as a Forward Air Controller (FAC)* in an Infantry Battalion or getting Permanent Change of Station (PCS)† orders to a staff job or schoolhouse.

I would spend six years in the Gunfighters; many of my peers had similar timing due to our operational tempo in support of OIF. During those six years the leadership in the squadron changed many times. I had four Commanding Officers and Majors (department heads acting as Executive Officer (XO), OpsO, and Aircraft Maintenance Officer (AMO)) who rotated in and out of the squadron every two years.

The squadron completed "workups" in preparation for each deployment. A workup consists of the training required to ensure the squadron is ready for deployment. Each workup involves countless days and nights of training flights to ensure the squadron's copilots, aircraft commanders, instructor pilots, and flight leads are properly trained and ready to accomplish the mission while deployed.

---

* Forward Air Controller (FAC): An aviator assigned to a ground unit who is trained to control aircraft conducting attacks in support of ground units.

† Permanent Change of Station (PCS): When a service member and their family are assigned to a new duty station; typically a move across the country or overseas.

We also conducted Deployments for Training (DFTs) with other units from across the Marine Air-Ground Task Force (MAGTF).* During a DFT, the squadron moves from home base to a location within the continental United States for weeks or months to train alongside units scheduled to deploy on similar timelines. Although you are still not deployed, you are away from home and in a simulated deployed environment focused on the mission with an increased operational tempo.

By the end of my time in the Gunfighters, I'd seen all of this play out so many times, seen so many iterations of the same ideas, that I knew which ideas were working well and which were not bad ideas, but posed efficiency problems . . . Well, okay, some of them were *bad* ideas! (Although I didn't understand it at the time, I probably spent about one year too long in the Gunfighters. I was feeling too much accumulated stress and had become too sharp around the edges, a sentiment I will cover in other chapters of this book.)

However, I learned important lessons in my last few years as a Gunfighter. I knew what was right and what was wrong, from *my* perspective. And I learned how to approach my leadership in a way that allowed me to accomplish someone else's intent, even if their plan was suboptimal, and still live with myself.

If there was a better way to accomplish a task, I approached my leadership with my recommendations. To be clear, I felt I needed to provide an alternative not because I wanted to get my own way, but because I knew life in an HMLA was dangerous, and I was identifying risks that needed to be considered. Risks I didn't have

---

* Marine Air-Ground Task Force (MAGTF): A flexible, scalable, maneuverable, and deployable command structure consisting of a Ground Combat Element (GCE), Aviation Combat Element (ACE), and Logistics Combat Element (LCE).

the authority to mitigate. My leadership needed to understand and accept these risks. The leader I went to was the OpsO. I would make a recommendation on how to get from our current state to the desired state while avoiding some of the shortfalls in the current plan.

The key for me was to identify a path to reach the desired end state more efficiently and with less risk. If my leadership wanted to try my way, great! They often did. If they didn't, that was fine too. I understood that my way wasn't the only way and just because I thought I had a better idea didn't mean I was right. If they chose another path, I would turn on my heel and carry out their intent as if it were my own plan. Otherwise, I'd risk being seen as Chicken Little, dismissed because I always thought the sky was falling. That was not me—leadership trusted me because they knew I would give my whole effort to accomplish the mission their way, with no degradation in effort.

But I couldn't do that without first speaking the truth. I just couldn't carry forward a task with unacceptable inefficiency or unnecessary risk without identifying it to my leadership first. I was lucky to have leaders who were willing to listen and who knew I was only trying to make the organization better and safer.

When you find yourself in a leadership position, inspire your team to speak truth to your power. Don't become the senior leader you avoided when you were a Captain. Your team will spend their time finding new and better ways to improve your organization and provide you with the opportunity to approve their plan and make the risk decisions.

Readback

To effectively speak truth to power, you must first become an expert in your field. If not yet an expert, you must have earned the trust and confidence of your leadership. Without those two ingredients, you risk coming across as a know-it-all and may be perceived as someone who always thinks the sky is falling. Your ideas matter! Identify a problem and a solution that results in a better desired end state with a more efficient, effective, and/or safer process. If your plan is adopted, execute to the best of your ability. If your plan is rejected, don't pout or take offense. Turn on your heel and give your best effort!

Never come back to them with an "I told you so." If you clearly communicate your plan to your boss, they will see the result and understand that they would have had a better end state had they listened to you. This will benefit you and your organization the next time you recommend an alternative plan. You will be seen as a team player and someone whose instincts can and should be valued.

CHAPTER 8

Don't Shoot the Smokey SAM

Own your mistakes!

The Commanding Officer is responsible for everything their unit does or fails to do. But what about the individual responsibility for members of the unit below the Commanding Officer? In this chapter, I'd like to address how someone who is not in command handles their own mistakes or failures. Other than the most junior person on a team, anyone in the Marine Corps will find themselves in some kind of leadership position. As leaders, at any level, we must take responsibility for our mistakes.

I have made many mistakes in my career, too many to count. Many were small and inconsequential to anyone outside my division or unit, others were significant and affected units outside of my command. After every mistake I've made, I attempted to achieve the following three things:

1. Identify how the mistake was made.
2. Don't repeat the mistake.
3. Own the mistake with my leadership.

One of my most memorable, and nearly catastrophic, mistakes happened while I was a student at the Marine Corps' weapons school, MAWTS-1. This is the school that makes our WTIs. WTIs are the core of the squadron's instructors, responsible for establishing and executing the training plans for all the pilots and crew chiefs. Only a few members of each squadron make the cut to attend the school.

At the WTI course the classroom instruction, flight planning, and flying requirements are all equally demanding and rewarding. However, any pain experienced while studying or during the grueling twelve-hour planning evolution is worth every minute of suffering because of the experience you get during the next day's flights. The flights are demanding and stressful but, short of combat, it's the most rewarding flying you can do as a Marine.

The WTI class has a building block approach with phases that expand from aircraft-specific instruction to missions incorporating all functions of Marine Corps aviation. This allows the students to crawl, walk, and then run during the six-week course. One of the flight evolutions at the end of the Cobra-specific phase was called Ninja's Box.

During Ninja's Box the students execute all the major missions expected of a Cobra pilot to include Close Air Support (CAS), Deep Air Support (DAS),* Defensive Air Combat Maneuvering

* Deep Air Support (DAS): Offensive air actions against enemy targets forward of friendly lines that do not require deconfliction from friendly maneuvering forces.

(DACM)[*]—the equivalent to dogfighting for helicopter pilots—with both helicopters and jets, and multiple fueling stops at FARPs. Students fly with each other with one instructor in an aircraft outside of the student formation. During my class the instructor was Major David "Spanky" Moore, flying as "high bird" to manage and direct the event from a distance above and adjacent to the flight of five Cobras. The mission changes throughout the event and each student is placed into a leadership role for the flight as the day progresses. No one knows what's happening next and the students must work together to achieve success as a team.

On this flight we had already changed lead[†] multiple times, conducted several strikes, and been engaged by fixed-wing and rotary-wing aggressors to include a Russian Hind helicopter. No shit, MAWTS-1 contracts a company that flies real Russian Hinds.[‡] We had just completed another stop for gas at the FARP and were heading into a range area called Mount Barrow to provide Close Air Support to a non-qualified Joint Terminal Attack Controller (JTAC).

A JTAC is a service member who is school trained to control aircraft during CAS missions in close proximity to maneuvering ground forces. They are some of our nation's best and most qualified personnel; their job is to take, and save, lives in combat. A

---

* Defensive Air Combat Maneuvering (DACM): A helicopter's form of dogfighting enemy aircraft; using the aircraft's agility to evade enemy fire to break contact or create space to engage.

† Changing lead: Transfer of tactical control of a flight from one aircraft to another as part of planned transition or in reaction to enemy action.

‡ Hind: A Russian-made attack helicopter with similar capabilities to a US AH-1 Cobra or AH-64 Apache.

non-qualified JTAC is another name for anyone on the ground who's in a firefight, has a radio, and has air on station to support them. In this training scenario, the JTAC had been shot and a random Marine picked up the radio to control the students participating in Ninja's Box.

Mount Barrow is located north of Yuma, Arizona, in a range complex known as R-2507 South. The impact area has a short dirt runway surrounded by many different targets—old tank hulks, personnel carriers, and tire stacks. Steep mountainous terrain surrounds it on all sides, limiting the visibility of attacking aircraft, unless they approach from an elevated altitude.

During Ninja's Box, several Marines were established on an Observation Post (OP)* to simulate engagement with the enemy at close range. Our job was to provide CAS. On this day, the ground forces were located in an OP to the northeast side of the range and were being engaged by mechanized enemy approaching from the west.

My flight departed from the FARP and approached the objective area from the north. My aircraft was the second in the flight, otherwise known as "-2." I was flying from the backseat and my copilot was a Marine named Captain Jonathan "Stryker" Bidstrup. The flight checked in with the ground force, and we understood this CAS mission was going to be more difficult, because a non-qualified JTAC was on the radio, and he was having a bad day. Major Brian "Trigger" Ashford, a Cobra MAWTS-1 instructor and a real-world qualified JTAC, was playing the role of the non-qualified JTAC with a bad, yet funny, Southern accent. He

---

* Observation Post (OP): A preselected location to observe enemy movement or action.

sounded frantic and asked us to immediately begin engaging the enemy with ordnance. Our flight lead was struggling to gain control and caved into the pressure from Trigger to push into the objective area before we had proper situational awareness.

Our flight was about to completely come off the tracks.

We were in trouble, but not solely due to Trigger's anxiety-producing pleas. It's never just one thing. In aviation safety we often refer to the "Swiss cheese" model, which states that for a mishap to happen, a number of compounding mistakes must line up as causal factors.* Picture two pieces of Swiss cheese where the holes line up in just the right—or wrong—way. If the Swiss cheese holes all align, people can end up dead. But if one of the slices of Swiss cheese can be adjusted during the event, the mishap can be avoided and instead of burying your friends, you can debrief the event, tell a funny story, or write a book.

Unfortunately, that year's Ninja's Box had several slices of Swiss cheese that were aligned to near-catastrophic perfection. Among our issues:

1. The student leading the flight had struggled during the flight phase and was not having a good day. The stress of a request for immediate CAS from a non-qualified JTAC didn't help him to manage the mission. We pushed into the objective area before we had all the information we needed to adequately support Trigger and his team.

---

* Causal Factors: The list of reasons, actions, or inactions that result in a mishap or accident.

2. Earlier in the flight phase, one of the instructors had burst into our planning spaces with a metal box in his hand. He slammed it down on the table and shouted, "Who the fuck shot this?" We looked at the 20-mm round* hole that had been shot through the center of the box and waited for him to explode. Instead, he smiled. He laughed! He wasn't upset; he was excited that the Cobras had shot the automated flash emitter box that simulated enemy fire from the objective area. High fives were shared by all, and we all felt great about ourselves. My takeaway? His reaction gave me the impression that emitters in the impact area were intended to be engaged.
3. We also used another threat emitter called a "Smokey SAM (Surface-to-Air Missile)." A Smokey SAM can be placed in the objective area and fired at attacking aircraft, simulating a shoulder-fired heat-seeking missile. It launches an inert projectile a few hundred feet into the air with a spiral smoke signature from the launch point, simulating what some Man-Portable Air-Defense Systems† look like in combat. The Smokey SAM can be launched via remote or wire-guided controllers. Remote control devices can be engaged on the range and wire-guided ones cannot. During this Ninja's Box, it was controlled by a

---

* 20-mm round: Fired from the AH-1W's three barrel Gatling gun at a rate of fire up to 750 rounds per minute.

† Man-Portable Air-Defense System (MANPAD): Shoulder fired, typically heat-seeking, ground-to-air missile designed to shoot down aircraft.

hundred-foot-long cable, but this wasn't briefed as a safety consideration before the flight. (The phrase I would use hundreds of times after this day— "Don't shoot the Smokey SAM"—was not part of the brief for Ninja's Box either.)

4. I had just returned from Iraq; it was 2007 and the war was still on. I'd only had a few weeks to transition from war to the WTI class. I had not fully decompressed from the stress of combat. My mind had not yet fully left Iraq and at my core, I was still in a combat mindset.

Okay, back to Mount Barrow. The flight pushed from our Battle Position (BP) toward the objective area. We had received a 9-Line, a standardized attack brief used to quickly pass targeting information from the JTAC to pilots, directing us to attack personnel carriers on the north side of the impact area. As we pushed from north to south, I was on my lead's left side. He began his engagement on a set of tank hulks along a dirt road. Before I was able to engage, the first Smokey SAM engagement happened, and I pulled off without firing back.

Before we returned to the BP, Trigger requested an immediate reattack on the same targets. I had seen where lead's rockets impacted in the target area on the first attack. Trigger made no objections to lead's first pass, so I became confident that I was tally* the correct targets.

---

* Tally: A military proword, or standardized phrase used for brevity, to communicate sighting an enemy aircraft or target.

On our second attack, I was once again on lead's left side as we attacked from the same north-to-south direction. Lead began engaging with rockets on the same tank hulk he engaged on our first attack. I picked another tank hulk to the left (east) and began my level speed change for my approach on target. With approval to engage, I pushed my nose over, armed my aircraft, set the proper torque, and placed the top of my rocket reticle at the base of the tank hulk.

As I began to put my right thumb on the small red trigger used to fire rockets, the second Smokey SAM engagement happened. The telltale sign of a MANPAD launch came from about a hundred meters to the left of the tank hulk I had in my sights. I didn't think; I reacted to what, in my mind for that one second, was a threat to my life and the lives of the members of my flight. I jinked the aircraft ten degrees left and fired six rockets into the Smokey SAM. To this day I give thanks to God because those six rockets may have been the best rockets I shot in my career. Each one flew straight and hit the point I was aiming at.

As I pulled off target, all hell broke loose! Trigger, without breaking character, screamed, "ABORT! ABORT! ABORT!" into his radio.*

My blood ran cold. I remember losing feeling in my fingertips. As I safed my master arm switch and began pushing back to the holding area, my head was spinning. The abort call told me something was wrong, *very* wrong! Piecing the last few seconds together in my head, the timing of the abort call, and the tone of Trigger's voice when he transmitted over the radio, I knew my rockets were

---

* Abort: The word *abort* in aviation tells everyone to pull off without releasing ordnance. If you're lucky, the abort call is given before ordnance is released. In other cases, it's to prevent the next aircraft from continuing the attack.

the reason for the abort. In that moment, I thought I just killed someone on the ground. Trigger continued yelling over the radio in his Southern voice, "I told you to shoot the bad guys, not shoot me!"

Once I regained my composure, I keyed the radio and in as monotone of a voice as I could muster said, "Trigger, this is Bleeder. Those were my rockets. Is everyone okay?" After what felt like a long pause, he came back up on the radio and told us everyone was okay, and no one was injured. The feeling of terror from the thought I had killed a Marine on the ground in training was removed from my shoulders. A true blessing for those Marines and for my soul. However, the fear that I had just made a fatal error was replaced with a dread that I had just ended my career and was sure to be sent home from the WTI class.

The flight pulled back into the holding area while Spanky and Trigger communicated over another radio and the training started again. The challenges of the lead student continued to the point where I was placed in charge of the flight. I assume this was an oversight from the instructors, as I was in no place to lead the flight, but I wasn't about to cry uncle. We successfully completed the rest of the requirements for Ninja's Box and returned to base at Marine Corps Air Station, Yuma.

When we landed, I went straight to Spanky and the lead Instructor Pilot for the MAWTS-1 Cobra shop to tell them what happened and to own the consequences of my actions. I told them each individually that my rockets were not off target, that I maneuvered my aircraft while in the attack to shoot the Smokey SAM. I did it and I owned it.

I was thankful that no one was hurt but fully expected that my career was about to end. I thought I was going to be sent home from

WTI. In my mind, the Swiss cheese holes that aligned to allow this to happen had no bearing on the fact that the near-fatal mistake was mine and mine alone.

I waited in the ready room, preparing to be sent home, while the instructors and the MAWTS-1 CO met behind closed doors. I didn't know it, but the AH-1 Division Head was going to bat for me in there; after a long discussion, I was allowed to stay. I didn't even down the flight.* Several factors led to me staying, but I'm confident that my ownership of my mistake was crucial to their decision. Later, the Division Head would tell me that I did exactly what Attack Pilots should do: I saw a threat and I reacted.

I carried this lesson with me for the rest of my career. I never missed an opportunity to brief others on what happened and to preach, "Don't shoot the Smokey SAMs!" MAWTS-1 carried the lesson forward as well, incorporating these lessons learned into all future classes. Although everyone might not know my name as part of the story, every other WTI class learned something from this event.

Most mistakes aren't as serious as "shooting the Smokey SAM." However, owning your mistakes is key to earning and maintaining trust. This will often lead to receiving grace from your leadership. If you identify the cause and don't repeat the mistake, owning the mistake can remove, or lessen, any of the frustration your leadership may have regarding your performance. It can remove the frustration, or anger, from your boss's mind

* Downing a flight: Term used during a training evolution where the student has failed to meet the requirements of flight.

during a discussion about what went wrong. They may be angry about the outcome of a planning product or the execution of a mission. However, if you lead with "This is my fault; my team and I are assessing how it went wrong and it won't happen again," you have summed up most of your boss's concerns in a single sentence and can get down to more important things, like guidance or additional tasks.

Equally as important as owning your mistakes with your boss is owning your team's mistakes in front of them. Internal to your team, you are the boss and should expect them to own their mistakes. External to your team, the team's failures are yours, at every level. When the rubber meets the road and the mistake is realized, you're in charge and the failure is yours. Your team will know the root cause of the problem and will do anything for you if they see you accepting responsibility for their mistakes in front of your boss. If you have their backs, they will have yours.

I've made more than my fair share of mistakes. Because of who I am and my personality, I have always owned up to my mistakes at work. This personality trait has worked in my favor, most of the time.

This technique also works with me when I'm in a leadership position. I have led at many levels, from a small team of planners to a Commanding Officer of an HMLA. When someone owns their mistakes, much of the concern I have about the problem and the person is diminished. I recognize that in most cases, the fault doesn't lie with only one person and others may have been the true cause of the problem, but if someone points fingers in other directions and blames others to get the focus off themselves, they will lose my trust.

Readback

Everyone makes mistakes.

Sometimes you're the only one who knows, and you can fix them yourself. Or, if you have an elevated sense of self and want to help others, you may share your private mistakes with others to help them to not repeat your failures.

As for the rest of us, most of us have a boss who will discover our mistakes even if we do not make them in their presence. If you want to maintain trust with your leadership and your team, own your mistakes. Do *not* point fingers at others—if you screwed up or your team didn't meet the mark, take ownership. If your boss is worth working for, they will see past the immediate situation and understand there are many factors leading to a mistake or shortfall. By owning your mistake, you provide an opportunity for your boss to skip past their first concern, your performance, and look at how they can streamline the organization, get additional support or resources, or even look within themselves to identify the mistakes *they* made to get the organization into this situation. After all, your boss is your leader, and they own the successes and failures of their organization too!

CHAPTER 9

Do the Right Thing at the Right Time for the Right Reasons

You're always being watched.

It's easy to get caught up in day-to-day life. To feel like you're moving along on autopilot, and you've become invisible to the rest of the world. In the military this couldn't be further from the truth. Your leaders, peers, and subordinates are watching you. Your family and friends are watching you. The American public is watching you. Understanding this concept can prevent you from missing opportunities and being left behind.

In the Marine Corps, your leadership is always watching you. If you are a Private, your Lance Corporal or Corporal are looking for the next leader in their shop. The next one to get a new qualification to help the unit be ready for deployment. The Captains are watching every aspect of the new group of Lieutenants, searching for whom to put in leadership positions and to be fast-tracked through the training pipeline to be the next NSI or WTI.

It doesn't stop there. The Majors are looking at the Captains to find who should be an OpsO or AMO and the CO is looking for who has the talent to be a Commander. The Marine Aircraft Group CO is looking to the squadron COs for someone who has what it takes to be promoted to Colonel and become a MAG Commander.

Your peers are watching you too. They want to know if they can trust you in your ground job, while planning for a flight, or as a wingman in combat. They want to know if you're the one they want to spend time with after work to hit the bars or if they can trust you with their real-life challenges. Will you help them navigate the challenges of caring for a sick parent, having a child with disabilities, or tending to a marriage that seems to be falling apart?

Your subordinates are watching. Those who work for you are *always* watching. How you act, how you treat them, how you stand up for them, can you be trusted, are you in it for yourself or the team . . . The list goes on and on. If you are a good person and a great leader, they will rally around you. They will bust their asses to make you look good and they will save your ass when you stumble.

Why does this matter? Opportunities to succeed and fail are tied to how you act and how people react to you. Your action may inspire all those in your sphere to greatness or, if your actions are less than inspiring, you may become a false role model who leads others down a difficult path. Never underestimate the power you have in the eyes of those who are watching you.

You may find the thought of being watched by everyone disconcerting. Some people feel like they can't function in a world where all eyes are on them. But in reality, no matter who you are, someone is watching you. It's an opportunity to be a good role model, to make them want to emulate you (rather than being an example of who they don't want to be).

Your actions can have positive or negative effects on your life, your job, and your relations. If you're a role model, your leaders will see it and place you in jobs that have a greater impact on others. On some selection boards, the board members who know you can be as important as your record of work. Be the one everyone knows and wants to work with.

The next chapter, "To succeed, mature into your new role," is a perfect example of someone watching me and taking action to help me become a better Marine.

Readback

It doesn't matter if you are the most senior or most junior person in any organization; everyone is watching you. It may be more true today than ever before—there are cameras everywhere. You are being observed for many reasons, depending on whose eyes are watching you. Your actions can catapult you to success, and they can inspire others to greatness. Or, if you're the antithesis of a good role model, they can be used as an example of how one shouldn't act.

Be a good person, make the right decisions, and lead the way you want to be led. Be an example for your boss, coworkers, subordinates, friends, spouse, and *kids* to emulate. Be the one who returns the grocery cart, holds the elevator door, or doesn't "double dip" the chip. If you do the right thing, at the right time, for the right reason, there is nothing you can't do, and you may be surprised by the number of people who will follow you to meet any challenge.

CHAPTER 10

At Some Point, We All Have to Round Our Edges

To succeed, mature into your new role.

Major "Ninja" Maduka was my OpsO. I was serving as the squadron's Pilot Training Officer (PTO)* and it was my job to get the squadron's aircrew trained and ready for their next deployment, this time to Afghanistan. I would not join them, but that didn't stop me from striving to make them as successful as I could before I departed the squadron I loved.

I'd known Ninja for some time, first when he was an instructor at MAWTS-1 and as my OpsO on my last deployment to Iraq. He had seen me at my best and at my worst. He knew if he asked me a hard question, I would give him an honest opinion. Years later, he would ask me to come work for him as his OpsO when he took Command of HMLA-367, "Scarface," and I would continue to

* Pilot Training Officer (PTO): A squadron WTI working for the OpsO to implement the Commanding Officers training plan.

learn a lot from him, but the advice he gave me as a senior Captain was some of the most important advice I would receive in my career.

I remember Ninja and I were sitting in a small office on the second floor of the Gunfighter hangar. The room was too small for two desks, but space was limited and every inch counted, so there we were. Having an office with a door and a window was a luxury, so you would never hear me complain about getting one of the desks in this office. He was leaning on the desk behind mine, and I had swiveled around in my chair to face him. We had recently moved back into our squadron spaces in Camp Pendleton after returning from Iraq, and we were catching up on squadron business. He got right to the point.

"When you get promoted to Major," he said, "you can't continue to act the same way. You can't be the fire-breathing Captain that crashes into every wall with direct and unfiltered energy. You'll have to mature and grow up."

His advice hit me like a ton of bricks. To be honest, I hadn't put much thought into what it would be like to be a Major. I was too busy focusing on the Gunfighters' current problems and had little—or allowed myself little—time to consider what was next. But from that moment on, my eyes were open to who I was as a Captain and how I would have to change my approach without changing who I was when, and if, I got promoted to Major.

Was I really a "fire-breathing Captain"? Not always. I wasn't a yeller, and I rarely raised my voice in the cockpit. I was hard on copilots who didn't perform, but my instruction was intended to correct the mistake and build them back up. But I had to admit I was hard and angry and had little sympathy for those who stole my time. I use the term "sharp" to describe myself because I had become too rough around the edges. In a figurative sense, I would unintentionally cut too deep. Ninja's advice inspired me to begin the journey of maturing into a field grade officer. Not a "Yes Man" like I had accused Majors of being while I was a Captain, but as someone who could lead without that sharp edge.

Those who have worked for me as a field grade officer have heard me say that they don't want to meet Captain Cherry. Captain Cherry is the young Marine who lives inside of me and often bangs against the walls of my brain to be free to lash out in unproductive ways. (Some might also see this as PTSD, but that's not my point here.)

After receiving Ninja's advice, I made a commitment to keep Captain Cherry in his box. I made a continuous effort to maintain a cool, calm exterior no matter what was happening inside my head. As a Major, Lieutenant Colonel, and Colonel—a field grade officer—I would not raise my voice, I would not run through the halls of the squadron (even if an emergency was actively happening), and I would not change the expression on my face when presented with the most difficult of challenges. I didn't become a different person, but I forced myself to approach problems and emergencies in a different way, with Captain Cherry safely tucked away.

Why was this shift so important? As a leader, if you overreact in a crisis, your subordinates will follow your lead. Almost like the alpha dog's mentality influences a pack of dogs, negative energy from you will spread to your subordinates. Those who might otherwise not have overreacted may follow your lead and make bad decisions. I could not allow that to happen.

On the other hand, I didn't want to—and couldn't—become someone I was not. Captain Cherry and Colonel Cherry are still the same person; it's just that one's sharp edges are exposed, and the others are sheathed. I recognize that, to some extent, "what got you here won't get you there," but you are still you. You can, and should, choose to mature, or evolve, in how you handle conflict, but I'm not talking about a metamorphosis. I have not tried to emulate someone I'm not; I've altered my reactions to better suit my role, allowing me to approach challenges from a new and different perspective.

You can do the same. Ensure that your maturation into a new role is based on a slight variation of who *you* are without trying to be someone you are not. Otherwise, those you lead will see right through you, leaving you with diminished authority.

Readback

Our lives are continuously changing. The changes can include attending a new school, joining a new team, starting a new job, or accepting a promotion. You could also start a new relationship, become a mom or dad, or transition to being a caretaker for an aging parent. It's important to understand that you may need to change your actions and reactions as you move into a new role in life. You may still succeed without making changes, but your success could be diminished if you don't take an introspective look at who you were and who you need to become or how you need to grow into your role. To some this may come easy; to others it will be difficult to acknowledge and instigate the change that is needed.

CHAPTER 11

Keep Your Foot on the Gas

Never off-ramp yourself.

Most people don't join the Marine Corps with the expectation to stay in for twenty or thirty years. I certainly didn't. I joined the Marine Corps to serve my country, test myself, and to be a Cobra pilot; I didn't think much past those goals until they were achieved. I understood I was accepting a six-year commitment upon completion of flight school, and I knew I would have plenty of time to consider my future in the Marine Corps when the time came.

As I approached the end of my first obligation to the Marine Corps, I had approximately eight years of service; two years to complete TBS and Flight School and six years in the fleet. It was time to make that challenging life decision.

And I couldn't make it alone. Jenny and I were soon to be married, and together we'd make the decision to stay in or get out. She and

I weighed the pros and cons of continuing as a Marine family or getting out and beginning life as civilians.

By staying in, I could continue doing a job I *loved* where I had already gained all of the expertise and credibility I needed to succeed as a Marine. On the other hand, staying in meant we were certain to move many times, which meant Jenny would have to start anew in her practice every two to three years.

By getting out, we could theoretically keep Jenny in one location to build her practice. But that prospect was quickly overshadowed by the distinct possibility that my next career could end up requiring multiple moves as well. On that path, I would be starting a new career, without experience or credibility, and we might still have to move . . .

One thing we knew for sure: We would only choose to stay in if we felt comfortable serving twenty years or more. If twenty years seemed like too long, it was time to get out.

Jenny and I ultimately made the decision to stay in at the eight- and twenty-year marks. Each time, we had long constructive conversations weighing the pros and cons. We decided to stay in because it was right for us, and eventually Joey, and because I was able to continue to advance and be successful in my career.

The decision did come with some conditions. We understood that for at least twelve years, many things would be out of our control. The Marine Corps would decide where we went and what job I would have. I had some say—those moves could be, and were, mitigated by my performance—but I certainly didn't get my first choice every time. After that, however, we agreed that Jenny would be in charge of what happened next—she would have veto power once we reached twenty years of service. At that point, her vote would outweigh the Marine Corps' vote. When she was done, we were done.

In the end, we were very lucky we decided to stay in. Had I got out after eight years, I would have entered the civilian job market in 2008, when the housing and stock market were both in free fall and no one was hiring. Had I decided to retire at twenty years, I would have been walking out of the Marine Corps and into the civilian world just as the COVID-19 lockdowns began. Fortunately for us, in both cases we made the decision to stay in before we could see and understand the peril of looking for a civilian job in 2008 and 2020.

I didn't join the Marine Corps with the intention of becoming a career Marine. I was open to options and if the right situation had come up, I might not have stayed in for twenty-plus years. However, I gave everything I had to the Marine Corps to ensure that if I wanted to continue to be a Marine, I was postured to succeed.

The bottom line? Work as hard as you can in every job you have. Take the right orders to the most career-enhancing job. Work so hard that your unit will give you the opportunity to get the highest qualifications and designations your MOS can offer. Compete to go to every career-enhancing school to build a résumé that makes you eligible for promotion or gives you the "tiebreaker" you need if only one slot is available for two or three equally qualified people.

Do everything you can do to be useful to your organization. Make the organization want to keep you above anyone else. Stay in the high-speed lane with an E-ZPass to blow through tolls without slowing down. If you do this, you can choose when you get off the highway, and you can choose your path.

If you look at your time in the military in two-to-four-year blocks, you have the opportunity to depart multiple times over twenty years. Additionally, the military has changed its retirement plans to benefit those who don't stay in for twenty years. The new retirement system provides you with retirement benefits if you leave earlier than the legacy twenty-year retirement plan. You have choices.

If you don't make a strong commitment, though, you risk getting offtrack and may become ineligible for promotion. If you're offtrack, you may be forced out of the military. If allowed to stay in, you risk continuing service at your current rank with no hope for promotion, limiting your job options, your progression, your paycheck, your ability to choose your next duty station, and your retirement benefits.

Readback

In today's world, loyalty between employees and employers is waning. Few organizations take care of their people the way they did in the past. Civilian pension plans are extremely rare, and employees change companies and career paths frequently. Even if they don't quit or get fired, they may shift into what social media calls "quiet quitting," where they do the bare minimum they can to get paid.

Treat all of this as background noise and do everything you can to make your current organization better and to become more marketable in your next job. Take advantage of every opportunity to get new skills or hone existing skills within your current company while building your résumé for promotion from within or to become more attractive to a recruiter or headhunter searching for talent.

Don't off-ramp yourself because you are frustrated in your current position. Become the most talented person you can be and keep your foot on the gas. If you are unhappy with where you are, continue to grind while planning for your next move. If you begin to stagnate in your current job because you're unhappy, you risk a lateral move into the next job, resulting in the same empty feeling from the view of a new desk.

CHAPTER 12

When Your Time Comes, What Will You Choose?

To be or to do?

In a book called *Boyd*, author Robert Coram details the life of an Air Force Colonel named John Boyd.* He was an extremely influential officer who played a huge role in the path of aviation and the Marine Corps.

Boyd developed the Energy-Maneuver diagram, which depicts an aircraft's energy state and maneuverability by comparing the strengths and weaknesses of different aircraft (US vs. adversary) in a dogfight. He was a leading voice in the development of future Air Force aircraft, specifically the F-16 and F-15. He also developed a concept loved and, in our minds, owned by the Marine Corps—the OODA loop. OODA stands for Observe, Orient, Decide, and Act.

* Robert Coram, *Boyd: The Fighter Pilot Who Changed the Art of War* (Boston: Little, Brown, 2002).

This was key to the development of the Marine Corps Maneuver Warfare* concept.

This chapter is not a book report on John Boyd. However, it does pull from his life and work by examining his philosophy of decision-making, which asks us to choose whether "to be" or "to do." In your career, you may be forced to make a choice: Do you want "to be" someone and ensure you stay on track for the next promotion, or do you want "to do" something, choosing what is right for your people, the organization, or your country at the risk of ending your career?

Choosing "to be" means you are doing what you are told, even when there may be a better way—ensuring you stay in good standing and remain on track. Choosing "to be" means you don't cause waves or make trouble at a pivotal point in your career.

Choosing "to do" something means making a decision to do what you think is right, at the risk of ending your career. At the fork in the road, doing what *you* think is right—*caution*, there is a chance you may be *wrong*, so be careful—may cause your career to go offtrack. Your decision to stand up for something can end your career progression. It doesn't have to, but it may be the last meaningful stand you will take in your career. If the issue is important enough to you, stand your ground and fight for what is right. But be clear in your own mind; if you find yourself in this moral dilemma, your "to be" or "to do" moment may have significant consequences. Never lose sight of that.

---

* Maneuver Warfare: A warfighting concept, inspired by John Boyd's OODA loop and used by the Marine Corps to disrupt the enemy's plan of action through rapid and violent actions.

My To Be or To Do Moments

These moments are, or should be, few and far between. Many will never be faced with this dilemma. In my career, I can clearly call out two times when I chose "to do" something. For the first, I had not yet read the book *Boyd*, but I had an innate understanding of what I thought was right, what I wanted, and that I was willing to do what was right, regardless of the consequences. The second time, I understood this concept and was willing to cap my career as a Lieutenant Colonel if my "to do" movement ended poorly.

Iraq

In 2007 I was deployed to Iraq for my third time. The war was still on, Marines on the ground were engaged with the enemy on a routine basis, and the HMLA Cobras and Hueys were shooting a lot. In addition to kinetic engagements, there were a lot of Casualty Evacuation (CASEVAC) missions. HMLAs provided armed escort to USMC CH-46 and Army UH-60 assault support or transport helicopters. These helicopters picked up injured US, coalition, civilian, and enemy personnel from the field, Point of Injury (POI), or from aid stations on a base or outpost and brought them to a location with a more capable medical facility or hospital. The Standard Operating Procedure (SOP) for an HMLA was to launch one Cobra for a routine mission from one Forward Operation Base (FOB) to another and two Cobras as CASEVAC chase if the pickup location was a POI.

POI transport wasn't a simple operation, because there was a high likelihood of enemy engagement. POI CASEVAC missions were routinely tasked after, or during, a Troops In Contact (TIC) mission. A TIC meant the US forces were actively engaged in a firefight with the enemy. In those cases, we would launch a section* of aircraft to support the ground force with CAS, arriving on station to provide aviation fires (missiles, rockets, and guns) and eyes in the sky to provide situational awareness.

A siren initiated by the Operations Duty Officer (ODO) alerted the aircrew and maintainers of a CASEVAC mission. Squadron personnel responded immediately—it looked like a scene in a Hollywood movie, as all alert aircrew and maintainers dropped everything they were doing and started a dead sprint to the aircraft. On this base, the run could be two hundred to four hundred yards from the squadron spaces to the aircraft.

The pilots arrived at the aircraft a few seconds after the maintenance and ordnance crews to ready the aircraft for flight. The pilots jumped in, strapped in, started the aircraft, and prepared to be armed.† The choregraphed play of highly trained professionals was so amazing, it was eye watering for me to watch.

The expectation was to be at your aircraft, started, armed, updated on mission information, and taxiing to join the CASEVAC aircraft in five minutes. There was also an unofficial competition to be ready to take off first. Not just because first was best, but because we knew that time was precious in these situations. When someone, friendly or enemy, is badly injured and needs medical attention, every second matters to the injured person's life and to

---

* Section: A term used for a flight of two aircraft working together as a team, each in support of the other.

† Arming the aircraft consists of removing several mechanisms that "safe" the ordnance and prevent them from being fired when you don't want them to.

their family. Our job was to be ready. The whole squadron moved with purpose, speed, and intensity that could only be achieved if sequenced into the expeditious, yet still safe, choreography of the CASEVAC chase mission.

The whole scene played out not on just one, but on at least two aircraft simultaneously. A CASEVAC requiring a single aircraft to launch required two crews running to two aircraft to start, with only one launching. The other crew was a backup in case the primary aircraft had a mechanical issue. If there was a POI CASEVAC, we would send *three* crews to their aircraft, allowing for two aircraft to launch and one spinning backup.

One day, the Gunfighters were redlined. We had three sections on alert to launch in support of planned General Support missions and TICs. We also had three Cobras on alert in support of CASEVAC escort, all single aircraft lines typically launching to chase a single CASEVAC aircraft, creating a section of two aircraft, one assault support, and one attack. The three CASEVAC chase aircraft would rotate through the primary, alternate, and tertiary positions depending on who launched last or who had already flown that day. As an example, if there were six routine CASEVAC missions, each crew would fly three times that day.

This day was busy with planned missions for our dedicated General Support sections. Two sections of General Support and two CASEVAC chase aircraft were airborne, leaving aircraft available to be tasked down to a single Cobra for CASEVAC chase and our remaining General Support section, consisting of a Cobra and a Huey. Hueys typically didn't launch on CASEVAC chase missions because of the UH-1N model's slower maximum speed. However, if a Cobra was unavailable, the Huey was in.

The siren sounded and three crews ran in support of a POI CASEVAC mission. I was the Primary for CASEVAC in my Cobra with my copilot First Lieutenant "BABS" Vogel. My CO was lead for the General Support section, he was secondary, and his wingman was tertiary in a Huey.

During the time it took to run to the aircraft, additional CASEVAC missions were received by the ODO. Our requirements went from a single POI, requiring two aircraft, to three separate CASEVAC missions. This was rare, a first for me.

Once my radios were on, I began communicating with the ODO; he had updated information, and it was time for us do that Marine shit. See through the fog of war and come up with a plan. It was my job to sort the crews for each mission.

Shortly after I started, the Huey crew checked in with the ODO for updates and I relayed the updated plan to them. Unfortunately, my CO's aircraft was turning but delayed in checking in with the ODO. Once he was up comms, I gave him the plan.

Yes, I was a Captain telling my CO, a Lieutenant Colonel, what to do. This may seem strange, but in this case, I was lead for the mission. My CO had the right to interdict and take action as he saw fit, but in almost every case aviators understand who is in charge in the aircraft, or on a mission, based on who is the "signer"* for the aircraft or lead for a flight.

We now had three separate missions and needed to send a single aircraft in support of each. The fog of war affecting the skid crews was also infiltrating the cockpits of the CH-46s crews, making the

* Signer: The pilot who signs for the aircraft before taking off, responsible for safety of the aircraft and crew and safe and effective conduct of the assigned mission.

orchestration of who was in support of what mission challenging for all. Difficult but not impossible. On the skid side, we had it sorted, I thought . . .

Here is where things got interesting, or should I say dangerous.

As lead, I was going with the first CH-46 crew to launch and would take off from our line first. My CO should have taken off second, followed by the Huey.

Before I go further, I need to paint a picture of how our aircraft are parked. Because we carry forward-firing ordnance, and in wartime, our mission-ready aircraft are always loaded with ordnance, we point the nose of our aircraft in a safe direction. There were large sand-filled barriers in front of each aircraft and concrete pillars in between them. In Al-Taqaddum (TQ), based on how the ramp was designed, we had two rows of aircraft parallel to each other. The aircraft in each row were oriented in the opposite direction from those in the next row. In a Cobra, there are two pilots and no crew chiefs. The pilot's visibility behind them is *zero* and when back-taxiing, we rely solely on our plane captains* to clear our tail. (This is less of a problem for the Huey because they have crew chiefs in the aircraft that can see behind them and are in constant communication with the pilots.)

To get out of our parking spots in TQ, we had to back up before being turned to taxi forward to the runway. Each crew understands that our tails are pointing toward each other as we come out of the line and are extremely cautious as we back-taxi under the direction of the plane captain.

---

* Plane captain: A highly trained mechanic responsible for the safety of the aircraft and crew before takeoff, and in this case responsible for the safe taxi to and from the line.

On this day, fate had my aircraft on the sister spot of my CO. We were tail-to-tail. It's not unsafe; while both aircraft are turning on the deck, there is plenty of room to back-taxi one aircraft while the other is on deck turning. It's not comfortable, for either crew, but safe, if all goes according to plan.

Here's how it's supposed to go: The plane captains know the primary, secondary, and tertiary aircrew through communication between the ODO and Maintenance Control. When the aircrew is ready to launch, a thumbs-up is given to the plane captain. The plane captain gives hand and arm signals to the pilots to safely direct them out of the line.

On this day, a combination of changing parameters for the mission, the confusion of the ODO and aircrew, and the inability of Cobra crews to verbally communicate with the plane captains led to a near-catastrophic mishap.

My plane captain signaled for us to lift into a hover and started to direct us to back-taxi to the taxiway centerline. The back-taxi distance is only about the length of the helicopter.

About two seconds into our back-taxi, our plane captain signaled for us to hold and land. His actions were sharp, purposeful, and he moved with intensity. I could feel the intensity in his motions and without hesitation I followed his signals and landed the aircraft.

As I set the aircraft down, I looked over my left shoulder and saw the tail of my CO's helicopter swinging through the airspace that my Cobra was supposed to be in. My CO lifted and back-taxied at the same time as me. Our plane captain saved my life, the lives of the pilots in both aircraft, and likely the lives of many maintenance personnel on the ground. The aftermath of a tail-to-tail mishap with two aircraft at hover power* would have been catastrophic, with aircraft parts and flames being thrown across the flightline.

I was furious! Happy to be alive but furious that my CO had lifted ahead of me. He was the Command Officer, but I was lead and that matters in aviation. With his aircraft clear, I gave a signal to the plane captain and lifted into the air. The CO was now in front of me. Still steaming, I asked him if he "had the lead" over the radio. Seemingly oblivious to what had just happened, he responded that I still had the lead.

It hit me that he didn't know I was parked behind him because he was moving too fast to comprehend the complexity of this mission. I couldn't believe he was doing exactly what he had explicitly directed the rest of us not to do! I had been in the meetings where he had directed the pilots and crew chiefs to slow down, explaining that we *cannot* rush. Moving too fast was going to cause a mishap. It was great guidance, but an underlying issue was *he* was known to rush and there were some other leaders in the squadron who followed his lead. On this day, he was rushing and almost killed me.

With him ahead of me as we taxied to the runway, the plan for who joined which CH-46 was off. I quickly reworked the order between the ODO and the three H-1s. Each flight of two, a CH-46 and an H-1, departed from TQ on newly assigned and separate missions.

My flight was the longest of the three missions. I was able to compartmentalize my concerns (read: anger) and accomplish the

---

* Hover power: Helicopters require more power, or torque, when hovering. Depending on the weight of the aircraft and atmospheric conditions, hovering may require the maximum performance the aircraft is rated to provide.

mission, but the fury came rushing back as we returned to base to land. Luck would have it that the parking spot closest to the ready room was open and I was taxied back into the line. As I set down, I saw the CO walking toward my aircraft. This is *very* unusual; it had never happened to me. As I set down and saw him coming directly for us, I told BABS, "Don't let me hit the CO!" His response was one of surprise and he asked me to repeat myself and I did. I said, "Don't let me hit the fucking CO!"

The ordnance crew had barely finished de-arming my aircraft and the CO was inside the rotor arch and standing on my ammo bay door.* My aircraft was still turning, and I was shocked to see him opening my canopy to talk to me. Communicating with someone outside of a turning helicopter is difficult, so I asked him to wait until I shut down. He agreed and stepped down from the ammo bay door.

My mind was racing. What was he going to say? What was I going to say? Did I really want to hit him? I was full of adrenaline, hands shaking from the totality of this mission and the near-death experience I'd stuffed away in a box in my head to complete the mission.

To his credit, my CO's intent was to immediately debrief what happened, take some ownership, and to apologize in his own way. I wasn't having it, I couldn't take it . . . months of frustration came pouring out of me. At the last moment, I tried to direct my words into a tactful response without losing the true meaning. I referenced the meeting where he told the ready room we had to stop rushing. I told him, "You were rushing!" I told him that his actions and lack

* Ammo bay door: A panel (or door) on either side of the AH-1W Cobra that provides access to the 20-mm ammunition storage. The door can be used to stand on while conducting maintenance, pre-flighting, or entering/exiting the aircraft.

of awareness almost cost the lives of multiple aircrew and maintenance personnel. That he didn't know who was lead and where the other aircraft were. That his actions were dangerous.

I knew that talking to my CO this way could be the end of my career. At that point, I didn't care and if offered a chance to do it again, I might change how the words came out of my mouth, but they would still carry the same message. I simply couldn't let this go with a shrug of my shoulders and a sentiment of we can do better. I had to tell him he was rushing, not just on this day but on other days. I had to "do" something.

I don't know if my actions resulted in making the squadron safer, but I couldn't go along with the way things were, I couldn't "be" okay with how this flight went and how some other flights had gone for others.

I was unsure for some time how this action was going to affect my career; I didn't anchor on the thought, but it was in the back of my mind. To his credit, my CO internalized what happened that day. So much so that every time I've seen him since, to include a social event fifteen years later, he brings it up. I don't know if he sees it the same way I do, as we are two different people with two different perspectives, but he remembers and uses it as a teaching point in his own life.

I hadn't read *Boyd* yet, but inside me was the Marine who couldn't just "be" and had to "do" when the time presented itself.

T-AKE

While in Command of HMLA-469, "Vengeance," I deployed with my squadron to Okinawa, Japan, as part of the UDP. UDP is a series of continuous deployments of units predominately from 1st Marine Expeditionary Force (I MEF)* on the West Coast to Japan. Units detach from I MEF and join 3rd Marine Expeditionary Force (III MEF)† for six-month deployments. While deployed, Marines are moved through the US Indo-Pacific Commander's area of operations to support Operations, Activities, and Investments (OAIs)‡ and to respond to any real-world contingencies, from natural disasters to crisis or conflict.

This was my third deployment to Okinawa, and I was cognizant of the "why" behind these deployments and the importance of our presence in the Indo-Pacific Command (INDOPACOM).§ My squadron's time in Okinawa was challenging. Some challenges were routine friction most UDP units face, and other challenges were unique to Vengeance.

Our deployment was also plagued by a series of typhoons. In a span of six months, we were impacted by twelve typhoons. None of the storms directly hit Okinawa, but each had a track that would impact the island. When a typhoon's storm track heads toward an airfield, aircraft are flown to a safe location or moved into hangars

---

* I Marine Expeditionary Force (I MEF): A Camp Pendleton, California–based Marine Air-Ground Task Force capable of deploying in support of crisis and contingency operations.

† III Marine Expeditionary Force (III MEF): A Japan-based Marine Air-Ground Task Force capable of deploying in support of crisis and contingency operations.

‡ Operations, Activities, and Investments (OAIs): Joint term used to categorize tasks that enable theater-level campaign objectives in support of the US Joint Force and Combatant Commands.

§ Indo-Pacific Command (INDOPACOM): A geographic Combatant Command responsible for the Indo-Pacific region.

for shelter. We had to "hangar the line"* twelve times in six months. That is twenty-four movements of aircraft in and out of a hangar. The total number of hours spent doing this was staggering, and every hour spent moving aircraft is one less hour conducting maintenance.

One of Vengeance's tasks was to deploy to Darwin, Australia, in support of INDOPACOM OAIs. The logistics behind movement of H-1s to Australia is significant. Not only does it require a long and manpower-intensive agriculture inspection (hundreds of man hours disassembling, cleaning, and assembling aircraft prior to an Australian inspection team showing up) but the H-1s don't have the legs to fly from Okinawa to Australia. The aircraft need to be moved via large strategic lift transport aircraft or ships.

Because of competing Combatant Command requirements, our strategic life aircraft fell out, leaving movement by sea as our only option. After significant coordination by higher headquarters, all the traditional options for sea lift were unavailable as well. Planners cast a wider net to solve this mobility problem, and our remaining option was a US Navy ship called a T-AKE.

A T-AKE is a cargo and ammunition ship with a single spot for landing helicopters. At most, the T-AKE can safely and legally hold two H-1 sized aircraft. My assessment of the number of aircraft required for my squadron to be successful in Australia was two AH-1Zs and two UH-1Ys. This would allow me to make a section

---

* Hangar the line: When a typhoon or hurricane is forecasted to approach within a specified distance of an Air Station, aircraft that are unable to fly to a location outside the path of the storm are towed into available hangars for shelter from destructive winds.

of aircraft each day with one backup for each type/model/series (T/M/S).*

My staff and I assessed the T-AKE option as a throwaway Course of Action (COA).† A throwaway COA often refers to a third or fourth plan that adds another option, but no one believes it's truly viable. This COA was even less than a throwaway. I fully expected it to be removed from the planning process.

I was wrong. Instead of being pulled, it quickly became the primary COA. I attempted to push back at the action officer level to kill the idea. I directed my team to work across all levels of the III MEF staff and across the Navy to highlight the risks this plan presented.

We ran into two problems. No one in our Service Headquarters, Marine Corps or Navy, would recognize or accept the risk associated with this COA. This left me and my staff in a very difficult position. The timeline for providing a confirmation brief to my MAG CO was set; my staff and I had work to do.

I assume my staff thought I was crazy, but I told them to plan this movement and provide me a brief on how we would accomplish the mission. They knew the risks; they understood that our Service Headquarters, those who could provide NATOPS waivers,‡ refused to act. They were aware of the Wing Operations Officer's

---

* Type/Model/Series (T/M/S): A naming convention to categorize US Navy and USMC aircraft.

† Course of Action (COA): Typically derived during one of many military planning processes, courses of action provide viable options for commanders to select in support of reaching a desired end state.

‡ Naval Air Training and Operating Procedures Standardization (NATOPS) Waivers: Granted on a case-by-case basis, exceptions to the NATOPS program requirements are typically approved when a specific requirement cannot be met due to extenuating circumstances.

comments, questioning our manhood as pilots, stating that he "hadn't flown in years and he could land a Cobra on this ship."

By this time, I had read *Boyd* and I had already been faced with "to be or to do" moments. I was prepared for this one. I also could not and would not just say no. I had one COA to get to Australia and I owed my boss a brief on how we could accomplish the mission.

My staff prepared the brief, and I tasked my OpsO with delivering it to the MAG CO. The conference room was full of my staff officers and Marines from the Wing and MAG headquarters. I wished it was a smaller group, but I wanted my department heads there because they needed to be in the room for MAG CO's decision, regardless of the outcome.

The brief was delivered, highlighting all the tasks, requirements, challenges, and risks. Once my OpsO was complete, I took the controls and drove my concerns home. I explained the risks again and I detailed how we were outside the box and would violate rules from at least two of our safety manuals. And how personnel across the enterprise who had the authority to waive the safety restrictions refused to approve a deviation but would not say no.

I explained to him that I could accomplish the mission, despite breaking NATOPS. I also told him we were writing the causal factors for this mishap from his conference room. I explained my understanding of the O5 Commander and how quickly the Marine Corps will fire me. I highlighted how there were many equally qualified HMLA Lieutenant Colonels who could take my job tomorrow.

"The Marine Corps doesn't usually fire its O6 Commanders, let alone its General Officers," I continued, highlighting that he owned the risk and it needed to be raised to the Wing Commander. If anything went wrong during this mission, I told him I wasn't the only one getting fired. He would be fired and so would the Wing Commander.

This point seemed to land as I had intended it to. I don't know if he was already there in his mind (I didn't think he was) but he soon delivered his decision:

My squadron would *not* be going to Australia.

I could feel the tension release from each person in the room. No one else had known about my plan, and the buildup to the MAG CO's decision had been intense. I'm sure it was a memorable moment in their careers. In fact, this story grew legs, and I've had multiple officers mention being in the room and remembering me for who I was that day.

I don't know how I would have felt if I were a staff member in the room. To be honest, I had tunnel vison walking into the conference room. I wasn't paying attention to who was in the back row. I felt the tension because I was choosing a moment "to do." I had a plan when I walked in.

I was thinking mostly about my staff. I wanted them to see that I had their backs. I wanted them to have something like this in their kit bags for when they became Commanding Officers. I knew they were concerned, and I needed them to see that I understood the problem and that I would be the one to push back on a bad idea. They did the work to develop a plan to accomplish the MAG CO's intent. We didn't say no because it was too hard or dangerous. We planned the mission and highlighted the risks. As a Commander, I owned the risk and it was my job to highlight the risk my leadership would assume if we executed this plan.

To his credit, the MAG CO listened to all sides and was keenly aware of the risk associated with this task. He made his decision—

that was his job and he did it well. Also, he didn't hold it against me. It could have been the end of my career.

Readback

Most difficult decisions fall far below the "to be or to do" level. We don't always get what we want and can't always have it our way. This is part of the normal ebb and flow of daily life.

However, on rare occasions you're faced with a true dilemma, a fork in the road. Do you choose "to be" a people pleaser and ensure progression in your career, or do you choose "to do" something and make a difference at work or in the lives of those around you?

If you're able to see your moment coming, you can prepare and spend the time required to assess the consequences of your action. Is your "to do" moment worth the risk of significant consequences in your professional or personal life? Is it worth making enemies? If you choose "to be" someone who goes with the flow, can you still live with yourself? Is a guaranteed promotion worth giving up a piece of yourself or knowing that you've left others behind?

If you decide to stand your ground, take the time to assess the consequences; otherwise you're playing a reckless game that can have far more damaging consequences than you ever expected.

CHAPTER 13

First Impressions

Don't be "the clown" on day one.

Joining any new organization is difficult, especially when you are just starting out in your career. Joining an HMLA is really difficult! The HMLA is hard on its young, its new pilots. You're scrutinized for everything you do and who you are. You are being judged, partly because it's our culture, but really because we want to know if you can cut it. Will you have what it takes to become an HMLA pilot? In other words, do you have the ability to make life-and-death decisions under the stress of war when your actions may result in taking the life of an enemy, or, more importantly, inadvertently causing the death of a friendly or civilian?

Judgment starts on day one and your first impressions can make or break you.

As a Major there were several things I told new pilots checking into my squadron. It was advice primarily for new Lieutenants but could have been helpful for someone checking into the squadron on their second tour.*

One key piece of advice was this: Don't be "The Clown" on day one. If you are the funny guy or the life of the party or there is something in you that showcases a *big* personality, don't lead with it.

Yes, everyone loves a funny guy, and in an HMLA there are many characters who develop the core of the squadron's culture. We love to laugh—at each other and often, at ourselves. (Well, we only like to laugh at ourselves if we are with our squadron mates, no outsiders. But that is a different story . . .)

But, if you join the squadron as someone with a larger-than-life personality, you better be prepared to live up to your own hype, because you are calling attention to yourself—attention you may not want.

The bottom line is that your squadron will put you through your paces, and if you come in bigger than life, you will be tested even more than most. They will apply extra pressure to you, and for good reason: They need you to prove that you're not someone who will end up killing the wrong people in combat or training. And with that extra-bright spotlight shining on you and your big personality, your weaknesses can become clear very quickly.

It's not easy to prove your place in the hierarchy of an HMLA. It's a strange world. So strange that when Lieutenants get promoted to Captains, other Captains will still treat them like they are of lesser rank if the newly promoted officer hasn't deployed or they don't have any qualifications or designations in the aircraft. You have to earn your place.

---

* Second tour: Returning to a squadron after completing an assignment to a non-flying billet.

So I always advised new joins, also known as "boots," to be quiet, hardworking, dedicated officers who are willing to help others in their time of need. I told them to demonstrate to the ready room* that they "give a shit" and help their peers and the group of pilots ahead of them in their progression during planning for their flights.

This guidance is beneficial for both the squadron and the new join. First, it sets the tone for the junior pilots and builds a sense of teamwork needed for all of them to succeed. But, more importantly for this chapter, it puts the boots on a path to success in this phase of their career.

If you call a lot of attention to yourself on day one, you may never shake the first impression others have of you. If you have a big personality, that's fine—be yourself, but be a subdued version for a while. During the first two or three months, put your head down and do your job. Slowly let your funny, or strange, or over-the-top personality out and the squadron will accept it and rally around you.

I've seen this show many times and it can go great, or it can go horribly. The point is, first impressions matter, and they can be long-lasting. Sometimes in a way you won't like and may never be able to recover from.

---

* Ready room: The location on a ship or within a squadron's spaces where the pilots and aircrew come together to plan and receive flight briefs. In this context, the ready room is a term used to describe the camaraderie Marines achieve when gathering together.

Readback

Imagine having dinner at a nice restaurant and the table next to you has one guy who is larger than life and cracking jokes, causing everyone else at that table to break out in a chorus of laughter. At the table, he is the beloved funny guy that everyone loves. To everyone else in the restaurant, he may be perceived as "The Clown" who has had too much to drink.

Timing matters, and when you become the "star" is key. When you join a new organization, the intensity of your personality matters in the first few weeks or months. Be yourself but don't allow the larger-than-life aspect of your personality to overshadow the hardworking professional side. Put your head down and do your job first. Once you've established a reputation as a hardworking professional, then slowly let your personality flourish. The organization will rally around you instead of building barriers to contain you or actively seeking to put you in your place.

CHAPTER 14

Find and Help Those Who Have Lost Their Way

Wandering in the darkness.

The culture of an HMLA is unique—we are hard on our young. Each squadron has its own take on the culture, but the expectations we impose upon our junior pilots are always significant.

Even in flight school, SNAs are warned about how hard it is to succeed in an HMLA. In the fleet, we push our junior pilots out in front of others when planning and briefing alongside pilots from CH-53, MV-22, and fixed-wing squadrons. Often an HMLA First Lieutenant will be briefing the escort* portion of a mission while a Captain, or even a Major, from another platform is briefing their portion of the flight brief.

This challenge is greatly beneficial to those who can rise to it. It makes them and the squadron better. If our junior officers can

* Escort brief: The portion of a flight brief where the HMLA pilots describe the plan to protect the assault support aircraft by destroying or neutralizing enemy threats.

plan and brief a complex mission, their understanding of what is required during execution of the mission goes up. This increases cohesion inside the cockpit and within the flight, increasing the level of trust across the flight and allowing each pilot to focus on mission execution. To put it plainly, by building trust in our copilots, we increase the lethality of the squadron.

We demand a lot from everyone. The squadron will push you, allowing you to get better at your job. In most cases this works, raising the overall effectiveness of the squadron. However, there are some who don't rise to the challenge. Those individuals sometimes get lost and may begin "wandering in the darkness." Some fall behind as pilots, others are great pilots but fail in their ground jobs, and some fail at both. This is a rare but significant shortfall in our culture.

As a Captain, one of my biggest frustrations was that once an individual crossed the invisible line from performing to failing, they were quickly left behind. I rarely saw an attempt to help them get back onto a path to success. The lost pilot would stop progressing in their qualifications, often leveling off as an Aircraft Commander[*] and Functional Check Pilot (FCP).[†] They were relegated to flying as a wingman to a strong lead during training and in combat.

If they fell behind in their ground jobs, they would continue to be given less and less responsibility. Over time, tasks that should have been theirs would be slowly taken away because they couldn't

---

* Aircraft commander: In a multiple piloted aircraft, designation as an aircraft commander is the first accomplishment as a Fleet Marine Corps aviator.

† Functional Check Pilot (FCP): A designated pilot responsible for ensuring an aircraft is safe for flight after maintenance actions are complete.

be trusted. Those tasks would be stacked on the shoulders of other officers.

"Never do a shitty job well" is a motto in the military for a reason. And there are some real shitty jobs in the military. Jobs that aren't in one specific job jar. They are pop-up tasks that someone needs to do, tasks usually spread-loaded across the squadron. Those who do the jobs well are often picked to do them repeatedly. Ironically, we seemed to be punishing success and rewarding failure. Those who are "wandering in the darkness" seemed to live by the opposite motto: "Never do your own job well."

This is going to sound awful, but as a Captain on my first fleet tour, I felt like the officers who were wandering in the darkness were stealing money from the government. They were getting paid the same amount as all others in their rank, but they were not doing their jobs. Why did we leave them "wandering in the darkness" like that? Why didn't we identify them and give them an opportunity to succeed?

As a Major and a Lieutenant Colonel, coming back to a squadron again, one of my goals was to find and help those who were lost. My goal was to ensure those who were wandering in the darkness understood where they stood with regard to their career. Did they know they were lost and didn't care or were they oblivious to the perspective others had about them?

If they knew they were lost and didn't care to change, that was on them. I would still work to motivate and set expectations for them. But I wasn't going to waste my time trying to lead them back into the light.

The ones I wanted to help the most were those who were lost, or on a path to becoming lost, and didn't know it. Bringing it to their attention was never an easy conversation. I'm sure it was difficult to hear and I know it was difficult to start, but I felt that they were owed the opportunity to see a reality different from the one they were currently living. I wanted to show them a path to success and provide them with the assistance they needed.

I identified a handful of officers who were wandering in the darkness. Most were junior to me but one or two were of the same rank. Two stories are worth mentioning in this book. Both were talented officers who excelled in their ground jobs. Neither were boots, and both had joined my squadron from another HMLA. And both were successful for completely different reasons.

One was a UH-1Y pilot, we will call him "Bobby," who was in a syllabus to become a section leader. In military aviation almost all tactical missions are flown in pairs, called sections. To lead a section, you complete a series of instructed flights to demonstrate your ability to tactically and safely lead a flight of two aircraft.

Before joining the squadron, Bobby had started, but hadn't finished, the section leader syllabus. The operations department planned for him to complete this syllabus after the normal warm-up and proficiency flights were complete. It was clear to the UH-1Y instructors he was struggling in the aircraft, and after several proficiency flights he indicated to his instructor that he was happy to remain a UH-1Y Utility Aircraft Commander (UHC).* He no longer desired to continue progressing in his designations and qualifications. This was a big red flag, and it is where I became engaged in his training.

---

* Utility Helicopter Commander (UHC): A designation allowing UH-1Y pilots to sign as the aircraft commander for tactical flights in training or combat.

I started with a detailed screening of his training jacket*, which revealed some startling past performance issues. The most dangerous was a near midair collision, where his aircraft almost ran into his lead aircraft during a nighttime training flight. This is always a concern in aviation, but it was especially raw because of a recent fatal mishap between a UH-1Y and AH-1W that ran into each other coming out of a FARP during a training mission in Yuma, Arizona.

I knew the pilots, both AH-1Z and UH-1Y, who were in Bobby's concerning flights. Because as an AH-1 pilot, I was not allowed to instruct a UH-1Y pilot from within the aircraft, I wasn't able to observe and evaluate Bobby directly in that case, so I reached out to the other pilots for more information. Their input validated my concerns and helped me to better understand the problem. The most shocking recount of a prior training event was a nighttime flight where the lead instructor in an AH-1Z remembered seeing the reflection of the cockpit instrument lights on Bobby's face as his UH-1Y flew across the nose of his aircraft with only feet to spare—just barely avoiding midair collision.

I developed a plan for how to approach Bobby and how the squadron could come together to get him back on the right path. During my first conversation with him on this topic, we discussed how he was doing in the aircraft from his perspective, his future goals, and his past performance.

I was firm and matter-of-fact with Bobby, highlighting what we could do to help him get past these issues and continue to

---

* Training jacket: A record maintained by the squadron operations department to capture aircrew performance, tendencies, and progress through each phase of flight.

progress in the aircraft. We could develop a training plan tailored to his needs. One that built his confidence and front-loaded his training in the simulator, placing him in his most challenging flight phases where he could learn, and make mistakes, without risking anyone's life.

It was a difficult conversation for me to have with him and even more difficult for him to hear, but I wanted to help him. I was certain he would take me up on my offer.

His initial reaction was different than I expected—he looked relieved. I wouldn't have been surprised if he had lashed out in anger, shocked that I would think so little of him. Or if he had told me he was offended that I thought he wasn't at the top of his game or that somehow I was missing something that could easily be explained.

But I wasn't expecting to witness an almost imperceptible relief come over him; it was like he had been looking for an opportunity to make a change in his life, but he couldn't find a way to take the first step. And now, finally, someone had offered a way out.

He wanted to take some time to think on what he would do next. Bobby went home and had a long talk with his wife about his future as a pilot, and they made the decision together. The next day he told me he didn't want to fly anymore. He figuratively dropped his wings on my desk. He was done.

I was shocked! We discussed his decision to ensure it wasn't a premature emotional response. It wasn't. I had uncovered a deep-seated concern he had been struggling with for a long time.

In the end, it was a positive outcome. Bobby transitioned into a non-flying job in the Marine Corps. He found success in a new MOS and, at the time of my writing this book, he had been promoted to Lieutenant Colonel.

The second example had a much different outcome. Captain Rob “Stache” Steinhauser had also joined the squadron as a junior to mid-grade Captain. He was already an Attack Helicopter Commander (AHC) and was in the section lead syllabus. He was smart, funny, and seemed to be dedicated. His transition into the squadron was on par with any other and there didn’t seem to be any red flags.

He and I were scheduled to fly one of his training events in the section leader syllabus. It was a unique flight where he was tasked to plan for and execute a mission with day and night times on station. The day mission was an escort of a section of heavy-lift transport helicopters (CH-53s) to an airfield on another island in Hawaii, and the night mission was an overwater shoot off the North Shore of Oahu.

It was a varsity mission to plan and execute for a young AHC, but he had plenty of time to plan and all the help he needed from other members of the flight. His plan was sound, the brief was good, and my expectations were high.

Shortly after takeoff, the flight started to go off plan and, as the instructor and actual flight lead, I guided the mission back on track to ensure we provided support to the training of the CH-53 pilots and crew chiefs while helping Stache stay in the fight. Nothing out of the ordinary for an instructed flight on a dynamic mission.

But as the escort portion of the mission continued, I was forced to hint, guide, or fix one small “pinprick,” or mistake, after the other. No one mistake would result in failure, but the small mistakes were adding up. I was helping too much and was beginning to get frustrated. With the escort mission complete, we flew back to Oahu and loaded our ordnance for the second mission while waiting for the sun to set.

The second mission started without incident but quickly developed the same issues as the first. At this point I was calculating the number of pinpricks in my head and contemplating if he was going to pass or fail the flight. The night shoot portion had no glaring errors and only small mistakes, but they were accumulating. He was falling behind in the flight, and I was asking him what he wanted to do next multiple times during the shoot.

He had the controls on the flight back to Marine Corps Air Station (MCAS) Kaneohe Bay. I was demanding as an instructor, but I was fair, and I did not look forward to failing anyone. I decided that if he was able to get the flight home, through the Combat Aircraft Loading Area (CALA)* and into the line without my intervention or guidance, he was still on track to pass the flight with below average grades.

Unfortunately, he was unable to finish the flight smoothly. On our approach into the landing to the runway and transition into the CALA, I had to come on the controls to fix his mistakes and avoid creating a safety-of-flight event with our wingman. Although this made my final decision easier, I was disappointed for him and the flight.

During the debrief, it became clear he didn't comprehend how much I'd had to intervene to keep the flight on track. That was an alarm bell for me. I didn't know him from before he joined the squadron and wasn't going to allow him to continue on this path without a conversation similar to the one I'd had with Bobby. Stache wasn't wandering in the darkness, but he was about to turn onto that path if he didn't change something.

---

* Combat Aircraft Loading Area (CALA): A designated location on a military airfield for the preparation and loading of ordnance on aircraft prior to missions.

After the debrief, I sat him down and explained that this performance wasn't going to kill his career. However, continued performance like this would quickly off-ramp him and leave him in a difficult spot. I was worried that he was happy to rest on his past performance and wasn't ready to put in the work required to continue. His response and attitude were exactly what I wanted to see. He received and internalized the constructive criticism.

This flight happened shortly before I departed the squadron to deploy as the Det OIC for a 31st MEU deployment to Okinawa, Japan. Stache stayed with the squadron and did exceptionally well. He would go on to become a WTI and, as I write this book, he is a Lieutenant Colonel and the Executive Officer of a MCAS.

I can't say that my interaction with him is the reason for his success. He was a smart and talented young Marine Officer who may have been able to find success without my intervention. However, I wasn't willing to miss an opportunity to identify, and attempt to correct, indications of a Marine who was showing signs of going offtrack . . . of beginning to wander in the darkness.

Readback

Life is difficult and not everyone has the opportunity or ability to be the best on their team or at their job. Some people's best may never be good enough. There are also people who choose to do the bare minimum to get by and are happy to be left behind. Others, oblivious to their place in life, unknowingly begin wandering in the darkness.

Anyone who has fallen behind or who is wandering in the darkness deserves a chance to make themselves better. Find those people and give them the attention and tools they need to come into the light. If you provide them with an opportunity and the tools they need to succeed and they choose not to put in the work to change for the better, their failure is on them. But if you don't attempt to help them come into the light, some of the blame for the failure of your team or organization will be on you.

CHAPTER 15

Can You Get Back in the Saddle?

Sometimes things go wrong. What do you do next?

Sometimes, things go wrong. They go wrong through no fault of your own, and in some cases, there is nothing you could have done to prevent a negative consequence from happening. I know this concept goes against many of the principles of Marine Corps Safety programs and the gut feeling of anyone who has been involved in a mishap or mishap investigation, but it's true: Sometimes things simply go wrong.

It's a fact of life for all of us, especially for anyone who serves their country through military service. They have chosen a dangerous profession and at some point, bad things will happen to them personally, or to someone they know, for no good reason. How they respond to these events, however, is in their control. Getting back on the horse may be the most important step in their recovery from an unfortunate circumstance.

As a Major I deployed to Okinawa, Japan, as a Det OIC of the Cobras and Hueys supporting the 31st MEU. After finishing my OpsO tour for HMLA-367, "Scarface," in Hawaii, I was fortunate to be entrusted with taking a team of outstanding Marines forward to Japan to support a MEU deployment.

Because of the deployment tempo during my years with the Gunfighters, all my deployments were land based, even my UDP deployment to Japan when I was a First Lieutenant. My first time landing a Cobra on a Navy ship was during my workup for deployment as at Det OIC in support of the 31st MEU. Unfortunately, time allotted for Scarface to conduct day and night landings on ships prior to 31st MEU deployments are limited, and I deployed to Okinawa without my initial night carrier landing qualification.

This fact was frustrating to me. However, I had a great team of WTI and NSI Captains who had MEU experience, and I knew I could rely on them to give me my initial night qualifications. Because of maintenance issues with the Navy ships supporting the 31st MEU deployment, I couldn't schedule my own night qualifications until we had already flown the squadron aboard the USS *Denver.* She was the oldest operationally deployed Landing Platform, Dock (LPD) ship in the Navy and paled in comparison to her newer San Antonio–class amphibious ships. The USS *Denver*'s flight deck was similar in size to the San Antonio–class ship, but all of the support equipment and hangar spaces were embarrassingly limited.

My detachment was separated from the rest of the MEU ACE on the USS *Bonhomme Richard (BHR).* We were alone but not afraid, even as we worked through communications issues with the rest of the squadron. We could see the *BHR*, but we had limited voice and data communication with her.

My time to get my night boat qualification and take one step closer to being a real MEU pilot finally arrived, and I was excited! I paired myself up with one of my Iron Captains, named Jonathan "V-Neck" Chaiken. We were scheduled to take off a few minutes prior to sunset. This would allow us to make a few landings during daylight and into "pinky" time. Pinky time is the period between official sunset and End of Evening Nautical Twilight time. That is when the light from the sun below the horizon is limited enough that you cannot see without the aid of NVGs.

An LPD has six different landing spots with options to land by coming abeam the ship and sliding across the deck to spots 3, 4, 5, and 6, or by flying from a quartering angle as you approach the ship to spots 1 and 2. On these spots your aircraft sets down with the nose at a forty-five degree angle from the ship's heading. Landing to spots 3–6 are far more difficult and congested, driving initial night qualifications to land to spots 1 or 2 to allow more room for error.

Landing on a ship, day or night, is a daunting task. A task that can be made more difficult by poor weather and high sea states. The pilot must account for the movement of the ship through the water, wind effect across the flight deck, limited visibility of the landing spot as they come across the edge of the ship, and a scan between a stable horizon and the pitching and rolling ship.

The Navy has Landing Signal Enlisted (LSE) personnel who provide hand and arm signals to helicopters as they approach for landing. They are responsible for the safety of the ship, the personnel on deck, and the aircraft. They also help to direct the helicopter over the spot and signal when it is safe to descend for touchdown. The final moments before touchdown are typically more aggressive on ship than over land because you want to limit the time spent at an altitude when the motion of the deck can come up and hit you while you're still flying. The "boat landings" are typically far more aggressive than normal land-based landings.

V-Neck and I took off successfully and conducted a few takeoffs and landings before sunset. The day was beautiful, and the sea state was as close to perfect as one could ask for. Noting that the sun was now below the horizon but it was not dark enough for NVGs, I gave the LSE a signal that I was ready to launch, and I departed the ship for another lap in the pattern.

My approach to the ship was smooth and controlled. Once over the spot, I watched for the LSE signal to land and began to descend. Because the seas were so flat, and because I was still learning, my touchdown was more like a land-based landing than a boat landing. After we were safely on deck, I told V-Neck I was ready to launch again. I raised my right hand to give a thumbs-up to the LSE to signal I was ready to take off.

Then, shortly after I had my hands back on the controls, it happened.

As I began to pull up on the collective, there was a loud bang, and the aircraft started to spin on the deck and lean back and to the right. I didn't know what was happening, but I knew I had to get power off the aircraft. While we spun on the spot, it felt as though we were sliding toward the edge of the ship. In actuality, the aircraft only turned ninety degrees before I was able to reduce the throttles and remove the rotational torque from the aircraft. I simultaneously rolled the throttles off and pushed the cyclic hard to the left to prevent the blades from touching the deck.

I yelled to V-Neck in the back seat to action the idle stops. Actuating this switch was necessary to allow the throttles to roll all the way off, past the idle stops. This built-in mechanism prevents pilots from inadvertently shutting down the engines in flight if they need to adjust throttle settings in an emergency. After a few shouts back and forth, I realized that I had such a strong death grip on the throttle that the idle stops were stuck. I had to let go of the throttles and ask him to cycle the switch again to shut down the engines.

With the engines off and all motion stopped, the rest of the world began to come into view. We were canted at a thirty-to-forty-degree angle to the right side of the aircraft. I can remember two of my favorite crew chiefs, Staff Sergeant Malm and Staff Sergeant Basan, and their completely different reactions to what they were witnessing. Staff Sergeant Basan saw what was happening and quickly stepped behind another aircraft on the deck, probably expecting a shower of aircraft parts if my blades touched the deck. Staff Sergeant Malm, far less intelligently but with selfless heroism, came running toward the aircraft before I got the engines off. He was the first one at my canopy once all violent motion stopped.

At the time, I had no idea what inspired Staff Sergeant Malm to run toward the aircraft instead of taking cover. While interviewing him as part of my research for this book, I found out. On a previous deployment, he was closely tied to a mishap that took the lives of the pilot and a crew chief while testing an aircraft over a lake in Iraq. The aircraft went in the water. The pilot didn't make it out of the aircraft, but the crew chief did. He saw it all happening again, to us: He thought V-Neck and I were about to go over the edge of the ship and his plan was to follow us into the water to save our lives. I get chills every time I think of this selfless act! I will forever be in his debt.

I remember putting my hands in the air like we do when the ordnance crews are arming and de-arming the aircraft. V-Neck and I asked each other if we were okay, and the team signaled the chain gang to come inside the arch of the aircraft to chain it down, with the hopes of preventing it from falling further onto its side.

Once we were safely out of the aircraft, reality began to set in. We were both alive, in fact everyone on the flight deck was still alive, but this mishap could have been devastating had our rotor blades touched the deck or the aircraft completely fallen on its side. If either of those things had happened, aircraft parts would have been thrown across the flight deck, injuring or killing others and damaging the other aircraft aboard.

Had that happened, Staff Sergeant Basan would have become the hero as one of the few bystanders left uninjured and able to begin providing lifesaving care to injured Marines and sailors on the flight deck.

While walking around the aircraft, I could see the right aft skid tube had completely severed—this caused the aircraft to rock back and to the right. If the aircraft configuration had been different, V-Neck and I would not have survived, and those on the flight deck would have been seriously injured or killed.

As it happened, we had an auxiliary fuel tank and a HELL-FIRE Missile Launcher (HML) on the right-wing stub. As the aircraft leaned to the right, the fuel tank and HML prevented the aircraft from leaning past forty-five degrees. This allowed me to keep the blades from touching the deck and prevented the aircraft from falling on its side.

Had those two wing stores been absent, I'm certain the right side of the aircraft would have touched the flight deck, allowing the blades to make contact at full power, creating devastation in every direction. Blades and aircraft parts would have sprayed across the flight deck, and the cockpit may have begun to pinwheel. V-Neck and I could have been thrown off the edge of the ship and into the cold and deep waters off the coast of Okinawa in the winter. Very few Cobra pilots have survived entry into the water, and those that have weren't able to exit the aircraft until it was twenty to thirty feet below the surface. Cobra helicopters aren't designed for buoyancy and tend to sink quickly.

After a short time walking around the aircraft to ensure everything was tied down and assess what had just happened to us, V-Neck and I went to get checked out by the ship's medical team and begin the medical side of a mishap investigation—blood work, checking for illegal substances, etc. The mishap aircrew also filled out a long questionnaire to capture any information that might provide a clue to the cause of the mishap.

Of course, the finger-pointing—on and off ship—began almost immediately. This was my first mishap, or, as we say on the helicopter side of aviation, my first "hard landing." For some reason it just sounds better. But no matter what you called it, anyone who heard what happened, via voice report or official message traffic, would assume that I crashed into the flight deck, causing the skids to collapse.

In my mind and in my heart, I knew that wasn't the case. But sometimes your mind tells you a story you want to hear and not the true story. The fact was that while I was at the flight controls of an aircraft landing to the flight deck of a Navy ship, I was in a mishap. The aircraft was still in one piece, almost . . . and no one was injured. I could live with the aftermath, no matter which way the investigation would go.

Fortunately for me, there was more evidence than my memory or the eyewitness accounts of the Marine and Navy personnel on the flight deck could provide. The old ship had a camera recording operations on the flight deck, and the VCR incorporated into the ship was working. My mishap was recorded. This fact may have saved my career. At the very least, it saved my reputation as a pilot.

The video evidence was clear that my "boat bounces" were safe and controlled. Just before the mishap occurred, my approach to the ship and descent to landing was controlled and safe. My final landing was far gentler than a landing on a ship could have been. My aircraft was safely on deck for approximately five seconds, and you could see the LSE lift his arms acknowledging my hand signal and telling me to take off for the next approach. At this point, the aircraft rocked back and to the right and began spinning to the right. We spun ninety degrees before we were able to get the torque off the aircraft and shut the engines down.

When my CO on the USS *BHR* saw the video, he could clearly see that the mishap was not caused by us.

But something had gone wrong. What was it?

An investigation revealed a key finding: There was a 2-millimeter crack in the aft cross tube. The crack was so small it had not, and probably could not have, been seen on any of the airframe's inspections. We had been sitting on a ticking time bomb and were lucky to have survived with no injuries and minimal damage. Within the next year, another AH-1W aft cross tube failed during a towing evolution by a reserve HMLA.

In the end, the mishap was determined to be a "Class C." This is the lowest and least costly mishap, only breaching the Class C mishap threshold because of damage to the lower wire cutter on the bottom of the aircraft. All other damage was minimal, and the aircraft was ready to fly again within weeks of getting the green light to begin maintenance repairs.

My CO's decision to put me back in the air shortly after seeing the video evidence was hugely beneficial to me and my detachment. I can't say that I was chomping at the bit to fly as quickly as I did, but his lack of hesitation to get me flying again got me back on my horse right away and provided me with the confidence I needed to continue to lead as his Det OIC. It also showed unwavering trust from him in the HMLA Marines. His decisive action, in coordination with the MEU Commander, stopped any finger-pointing from within the detachment and allowed us to move forward with our mission.

Readback

Life isn't fair and sometimes it will bring you to your knees with no warning. Regardless of how you end up in an unfortunate and unforeseen circumstance—whether it's through your own actions, the actions of others, or fate—how you respond to this adversity will determine your future. It will determine your self-worth and how you are perceived by others.

You may not be fortunate enough to have a leader who orders you to begin flying before you think you're ready. Even so, you must get back on your horse as soon as possible, in many cases before you think you're ready. This is especially true if you are in a leadership position. Pick your head up and press on! You're always being watched and your actions when recovering from adversity can inspire those around you or cause them to lose faith in you. It's your choice; what are you going to do?

CHAPTER 16

How Close Have You Been to Being Fired?

Trust but verify.

As a leader in the Marine Corps, trust in others is key to success. You need to trust your leadership, your peers, and your subordinates to do their jobs well to ensure the unit succeeds. Without trust in others' ability to do their jobs in higher, adjacent, or subordinate lanes, the unit becomes less effective, and in the Marine Corps, that could cost lives. This chapter will focus on how to develop trust in subordinates, captured by the often-used phrase: "Trust but verify."

Having blind trust in those who work for you is dangerous. On rare occasions, it's warranted—I've had Marines working for me who needed no supervision or verification, who were absolute professionals and better at their jobs than I was. Unfortunately, those Marines are rare, and most Marines need both trust and verification. It doesn't matter if you are leading the top or bottom 1 percent; it behooves you and your unit to provide the same supervision and verification. Your top performers will benefit because you care about what they are doing, and your bottom performers will benefit because they will receive additional guidance and learn what right looks like. Either way, you and your unit will be better when you trust but verify.

As a Major, I was selected to be an Aide-de-Camp to the Commander of Marine Corps Forces, Pacific (MARFORPAC), Lieutenant General John Toolan. I had completed my department head time* in a squadron as the OpsO and Officer in Charge of an HMLA Detachment aboard the 31st MEU. I knew a lot about the inner workings of an HMLA. I knew the people, the mission, and what was expected of everyone above, with, and subordinate to me. I understood when and where I needed to engage to verify what was right and wrong within a squadron.

As an Aide, though, I was new to the world of working for a three-star General at a level of Command I only knew of via many layers of Marine Corps command structure. At the squadron level, I had Commanders in the MAG, Marine Aircraft Wing (MAW), and MEF between me and MARFORPAC; I was new to the roles and responsibilities of an Aide; and it took me a little too long to begin to trust my instincts and trust but verify when things didn't seem right.

In 2014, travel of US General Officers to China was rare. For the Marine Corps, one way to travel to China was via an invitation to be the guest of honor at a Marine Corps Birthday Ball held by

---

* Department head time: Key Major's billets within the squadron critical to a Marine's competitiveness for promotion. Critical billets include: Operations Officer (OpsO), Aircraft Maintenance Officer (AMO), Detachment Officer in Charge (Det OIC), and Executive Officer (XO).

the US Embassy in China. In most countries, the Marine Corps Birthday Ball is sponsored and run by the Marine Embassy Security Guards. It's often one of the biggest social events of the year for diplomats from each country's embassy in that nation. Because of this, the Marine Corps sends its General Officers forward to participate in the many Marine Corps Birthday Balls across the world.

In 2014, Lieutenant General Toolan was invited to be the guest of honor for the US Embassy, Beijing, Marine Corps Birthday Ball. A rare opportunity he would not pass up in his first year in Command of MARFORPAC. As you might imagine, entry requirements for US military personnel into China are strict. Unlike many other nations, China requires a stamped visa in your passport before arriving. It can't be done online or in person when you arrive in the country. Our official passports had to be mailed from Hawaii to the Chinese Embassy in Washington, DC.

This doesn't happen without significant planning to ensure the passports for the traveling party are packaged and sent in time to be processed by the embassy and returned to Hawaii in time for our travel to China.

Luckily for me, the previous Commander of MARFORPAC attended the Beijing ball in 2013, and a Staff Section Marine who worked for me had handled the visas. He was still on the staff, so we had all the planning products and timelines from the previous year. We began working the timelines as soon as Lieutenant General Toolan decided he would attend the ball.

The Beijing ball was scheduled for early November, even though the Marine Corps birthday is 10 November, and every Marine will make sure you know it's the Marine Corps' birthday on that date. However, because of the number of units and the limited locations where a large ball can be held, Marines celebrate their birthday from late October through mid-November.

To ensure we received the visas on time, we sent official passports to a courier in Washington, DC, six weeks before our departure. The courier was responsible for receiving the passports in the mail, delivering them to the Chinese Embassy, retrieving the passports with stamped visas, and mailing them back to us in Hawaii. Not understanding the role of this individual was my first mistake. I thought he was responsible for hand-carrying the passports through the process.

Two weeks after we sent the passports away, I asked my Gunnery Sergeant for the status of the visas. After contacting the courier, he told me we were on track with no issues. Aside from asking for this status update, I was blindly trusting my Gunny in this process.

The life of an Aide is busy, and I was juggling many other tasks, timelines, and daily requirements. I couldn't and shouldn't have been singularly focused on any one task, so it's no surprise I wasn't singularly focused on the visas. But that turned out to be my second mistake.

Three weeks away from our trip, I asked again and got the same response from the courier via the Gunny. Alarm bells should have started going off. I could hear a noise in the distance (in the back of my head), but I discarded the concern and put my head down to accomplish my other tasks.

Before each trip, the G-5 (our plans and international affairs branch) put together two briefs for Lieutenant General Toolan. The first was a pre-brief that allowed him to shape the trip and the second was a final brief confirming the plan and any engagements with US and host nation leadership in each country.

The pre-brief was scheduled two weeks before our departure to China. After the G-5 gave their updates, I gave an update on all the travel tasks I was responsible for. This was the first time Lieutenant General Toolan heard that we were still waiting on the visas. He looked at me out of the corner of his eye but didn't say anything.

Trust was no longer enough. It was time to start verifying the shit out of this trip.

The first thing I did when I walked out of that meeting was to talk to my Gunny about the visas. He gave me the same update on the visas: "No issues." I told him I wanted the name and number of the courier. Because of the time difference between Hawaii and the East Coast, I couldn't speak to him until the next day.

Now I was engaged, but I had not switched into emergency mode. In hindsight, I should have started flipping tables at this point, but I didn't. This was my third mistake.

When I finally spoke to the courier, my little Aide world came crashing down around me. I realized the courier wasn't walking the passports through the visa approval process. He simply received the passports, delivered them to the Chinese Embassy, picked them up from the embassy, and mailed them back to us. He did nothing else. *Nothing!* Every update I received over the past month came from my Gunny calling this individual. There were no issues reported because the response was built on the incorrect assumption that the passports had been delivered to the Chinese Embassy. But I was less than two weeks from departing for China and I had *no idea* where the passports were in the approval process. The updates were useless.

I was desperate and didn't know where to go or how to work around the time difference between Hawaii and the East Coast, which plagued me. If I didn't get something done before 1030

(10:30 a.m.) in Hawaii, chances were I would have to wait until the next day to get a response. Every hour counted at this point.

Now twelve days from departure, I woke up at 0200 (2:00 a.m.) in Hawaii to maximize my coordination on the East Coast. The day prior, I had conducted a Google search for the State Department's China desk in Washington, DC. In my mind I can still see the large Hawaiian clouds overhead and feel the wind on my face as I stood outside my house in Lanikai, trying not to wake up my wife and son as I released the Cobra pilot inside me.

I had my first mini miracle when someone from the State Department answered the phone. The woman who answered quickly understood the problem. She was not only willing to help, but she also had recommendations on how to energize the process from multiple levels, including a recommendation to call the US Embassy in China for their assistance and pressure between embassies.

After coordination with the MARFORPAC G-5 and waiting until afternoon in Hawaii, I contacted the Marine Attaché at the US Embassy in China. He also understood the problem and was ready and willing to engage to find a solution. I now had individuals in China and Washington, DC, engaged in getting our visa approved.

The countdown continued.

Eight days from departure, the problem with our visas was identified. For more than two weeks, our visas had been waiting on final approval in the Chinese Embassy. They were literally sitting on the desk of the Chinese official with final approval authority. I have a theory for why they sat so long but, because I have no proof, I will keep that part to myself.

With pressure from the State Department and the US Embassy in China, the visas were approved and began routing back out of the Chinese Embassy in Washington, DC.

The final brief before our Thursday departure was given to Lieutenant General Toolan on a Tuesday. I still did not have the visas. During this brief, I told him that I was working on the problem and would give him any updates I had. He was not happy.

When staff members greeted him on his way to his next brief, asking him how his day was going, he said, "I'm good but I might need a new Aide."

He liked to joke around, but this was no joke. My career was dangling in the wind. Getting fired as an Aide was a sure way to stop any career progression; I was close to ending my career as a Major.

On Wednesday morning, I received the FedEx tracking number for the visas. They were scheduled for delivery on Thursday morning. You read that correctly: The visas were scheduled for delivery to Hawaii on Thursday morning. Our direct flights to Beijing departed at 2000 (8:00 p.m.) on Thursday. Without visas, we do not board the flight, and if we don't depart on time, Lieutenant General Toolan will miss the Marine Corps Birthday Ball. I'm now hours away from setting up my boss for a strategic failure.

I woke up multiple times in the night to check the status of the package with FedEx, and I was confident the visas would arrive in Hawaii on Thursday. However, there was still a good chance the package would not make it to the MARFORPAC Headquarters aboard Camp Smith on time.

I refused to leave anything else in this process up to chance. I sent my Staff Sergeant to the FedEx office at the airport to sit and wait for the package to arrive. He arrived in the office and immediately began making friends with (sweet-talking) the Auntie (a Hawaiian term of respect and affection used to address older women) working at the reception desk. He explained that we were waiting for a package and that we couldn't wait for it to be sent out for delivery. After about an hour waiting, the receptionist called out for "Ryan Cherry," and my Staff Sergeant, not Ryan Cherry, said "Yes, ma'am," and got his hand on our visas.

By 1300 (1:00 p.m.) on Thursday, my Staff Sergeant was back in the office and I had the visas in hand, three and a half hours before we were scheduled to depart for the airport!

By the time we got to the airport, I felt like I had aged ten years over the past four weeks. Still, there was one more moment of "glory" waiting for me. While checking in for our flight, the ticket agent took one look at the visa stamp and her jaw dropped.

> "Where was this visa stamped?" she asked.
> "In Washington, DC," I replied.
> "But these were stamped *yesterday*!"
> "Thank you, ma'am, I'm aware of when the visas were stamped," I said.

I could hear Lieutenant General Toolan laughing behind me.

Lieutenant General Toolan's laughter didn't stop at the airport, either.

During his speech as the guest of honor for the Ball, Lieutenant General Toolan diverted slightly from his prepared remarks as he took the stage. He couldn't pass up the opportunity to tell the story of how his Aide almost got fired because of the visas for this trip. Although we never discussed it in depth, he had seen the lengths I'd gone to to ensure the visas were delivered on time. He even asked me to stand up for everyone to see me, telling them I'd had a rough few weeks but I pulled off a miracle breaking loose the visas from the Chinese Embassy in Washington, DC. He told the audience to buy me a drink if they had a chance, because I needed and deserved one! There's nothing like getting roasted by your boss in front of a banquet hall full of diplomats.

Had I gotten over my own insecurities of learning a new job and listened to the alarm bells in the back of my mind, I might have been able to avoid the worry of being fired and ending my career progression. It didn't feel right and I knew it, but I failed to act until it was (almost) too late. Trust in your staff but verify their actions to ensure mission accomplishment.

Readback

Trust in others is a cornerstone to success in any organization or relationship, personal or professional. Without trust in others, productivity within the organization and maturity of relationships will be difficult to maintain and improve. However, if you are a leader, you can't assume your subordinates are implementing your tasks properly or that they truly understand your guidance and intent. You can't put your head in the sand and wish away the variables that may be key to the success or failure of your team.

If you're new to leadership roles or new to an organization, it may be difficult to take the sometimes intrusive steps to verify that work is being done correctly and on time. Push your insecurities aside and take the steps needed to supervise your team. You will find that some people need less supervision, and others may need constant interaction, motivation, and verification. Start now because the longer you wait, the harder, and more intrusive, it will be to develop a new rhythm within your team.

CHAPTER 17

Sometimes You Will Be Uncomfortable

Your way isn't the only way.

After finding success in the military, it is reasonable to assume the techniques you used to achieve your success are the best techniques. But as a leader, believing this can be a mistake. One that will cause you to miss opportunities to grow as a leader and to help others grow.

Your organizational and leadership styles work for you and can inspire others, but that doesn't mean your way is the only way to achieve success. It's not. You must allow your subordinates the freedom and opportunity to achieve your desired end state in their own way.

My road to command of HMLA-469, "Vengeance," was anything but typical. I was slated to command another unit but was offered the opportunity to take command of Vengeance on short notice. I was working as a Current Operations Officer in HQMC's PP&O in the Pentagon. It was an important and career-enhancing job, but it was a miserable grind, and I was ready to depart the Pentagon at the earliest opportunity. My chance to leave early came via a TANDBERG (a classified video teleconference system) call from the Executive Assistant to the Deputy Commandant, PP&O. He jokingly asked me if I wanted to depart from the Pentagon early. I knew I was on a short list, and when I asked if he was calling about Vengeance, he said yes. He was tasked with informing me that I was selected to command Vengeance. After talking to Jenny, we agreed to take the offer and our journey back to Camp Pendleton, and command of an HMLA began.

Vengeance was in a nonstandard transition. The outgoing CO had transitioned out of Command in time to attend TLS, and the slated inbound CO had been fired before he arrived. The MAG Commander asked a friend of mine, who had already completed his time as a CO of an HMLA and had already had his retirement ceremony, to become the interim CO to allow me time to move from the Pentagon to Southern California. Lieutenant Colonel "Fredo" Federico assumed command and led the squadron for about two months. During his time in Command, he used his experience and innate leadership style to make great improvements to the squadron, setting me up for success upon my arrival.

He made several changes and infused the squadron with his brand of leadership. Because he would only have command for a short time, he didn't make major structural changes to the squadron, including the operations division, the S-3, which sorely needed some changes.

I knew Operations inside and out; I spent most of my time in an HMLA in Operations. From First Lieutenant through Major, I held almost every job within the S-3 from schedule writer to OpsO.

I had seen and done about everything you can imagine in Ops. I knew what worked for me and how I wanted my operations division to be organized.

When I took command, the Vengeance operations division was not organized or run the way I would have set it up. If fact, I hated it. Fredo and I had spent so much time together in squadrons as we grew up, he knew I was going to hate it too. In our turnover, he said he wanted to change it but knew that was my responsibility. He didn't want to make changes I might undo, which would create undue turmoil in an already difficult transition.

My OpsO was Major "Nose" Smyth. He and I knew each other from my time in the Gunfighters, he had a great reputation, and I was lucky to have him. As a Captain, he had spent time in Vengeance, and I knew he took pride in the squadron and the organization of the operations division. After a short time in Command, I had an honest and open conversation with him about what I thought of the organization of his shop. I told him I didn't like it and I thought it could be done in a better, more efficient way. To his credit, he fought for what he thought was right and told me he could deliver my desired end state with the current design. He fought for his system and his people, and I listened.

I was candid with him—I might have even said I "hated" the way Ops was run. But I also told him I would be patient and allow him to continue with a few conditions. I told him the results I wanted and a date I wanted to reach my desired end state. If he could get there on my timeline, I would back off and the shop was his to run.

The goal I set for him didn't give him a lot of time to get there. To his credit, he not only met my expectations; he exceeded them.

He exceeded our end-of-fiscal-year flight hour requirements and cemented the structure of the operations division in my squadron. I was proud of him and his team for their win while still a little sad a part of my squadron was called "middle-ops," a name which conjures images from *The Lord of the Rings . . .*[*]

As a leader, you may experience times when your way is the only way, but those moments should be rare, only arising when you need to reach down into a department to fix a problem that can't be fixed another way. I wanted to demonstrate my trust in my subordinate leaders, to allow them the ability to achieve my intent and desired end state in their own way. This is key for several reasons: It demonstrates trust, allowing them to lead from their position; it takes a task from your plate; and it is a tenet from Marine Corps Doctrine, MCDP 1 "Warfighting."

If your leaders can drive the organization "down and in" without your heavy hand, you are able to focus your limited time on other problems. You have time to fix issues that need your direct attention, and to look "up and out." You can look into the future and above your organization to identify problems at a distance that you can influence before they become an emergency.

Trust your leaders. If they're competent, allow them the room to accomplish tasks in their own way. This may be uncomfortable and if you allow your insecurities to surface, it may make you feel like you lost an important battle. But when your team succeeds, you succeed.

---

* Middle-Ops: In addition to the traditional future and current operations sections, the Vengeance S-3 has a bizarre entity called "middle-ops" that is not codified in any doctrinal publication and that evokes the fictional setting of Middle-Earth in J.R.R. Tolkien's books *The Lord of the Rings* and *The Hobbit.*

Readback

It's hard to hear, but your way isn't the only way to complete a task. If you're an expert in your field, or just a control freak, it's hard to give others the freedom to complete your tasks in a way that you didn't design and don't have complete control over. As a leader of an organization, there will come a time when you need to allow others to experiment and grow by ensuring they know what to do without you telling them how to do it.

If you set boundaries and goals, you can take a step back and allow your staff to establish their own path to accomplish your goals. It will be uncomfortable; you may never truly feel good about it, but your staff will benefit, and their success is your success! Demonstrating trust in them will allow them to spread their wings and grow in their role. They will feel freer to lead their own staff, developing as leaders themselves. And you never know, the diversity of thought discovered when you step back from direct control may result in a far better end state than the one you could have achieved with everyone aligned and doing it your way.

CHAPTER 18

Are You Listening?

The Marine Corps is always communicating with you.

A Marine should never be surprised by the decision of a selection board for promotion, command, or school.* It's impossible to *know* the outcome, but you should never be entirely surprised. Even if the probability is 51 percent, you have tools to understand where you stand in the eyes of the Marine Corps and the members of the board.

Throughout my career I've been fairly confident going into a board, at least 51 percent confident. As a Captain looking for promotion to Major, I knew I'd done everything I could have done. My Fitness

---

* Marine Corps Boards: The Marine Corps promotion, command selection, and school selection boards assess Marines for advancement in rank, selection to positions of leadership and command, and attendance in formal military schools. These boards are formalized procedures that evaluate individual performance, potential, and qualifications based on a variety of criteria.

Reports (FITREP)[*] were outstanding, I had all the qualifications I could have as a Cobra pilot, and I had multiple combat deployments.

As a Major, looking at promotion to Lieutenant Colonel, I was far less confident but certainly above 51 percent. Competition for promotion to Lieutenant Colonel in the HMLA is fierce. There are far too many qualified Cobra and Huey pilots for far too few billets.[†] Many HMLA Majors, who may have been promoted from another MOS, were not selected for promotion. I was relieved and excited when I found out I was going to be promoted again.

As a Lieutenant Colonel (select) hoping to be picked for command of an HMLA, my expectations continued to diminish. I had a very strong profile and was very competitive. I had two department head tours as OpsO and Det OIC and a deployment on the 31st MEU. I was ILS complete, I had a successful tour as an Aide-de-Camp, and I was on a staff tour in the Pentagon.

My performance as a Major was excellent, but I was still worried because I knew that competition for an HMLA Command is formidable—the selection rate is about 8 percent. In the end, I was selected for Command but not for an HMLA. It was a sour pill to swallow but I wasn't surprised. I was ecstatic to be selected for any Command and was excited to head back to Southern California to take over as the CO for Headquarters & Headquarters Squadron (H&HS) at MCAS Camp Pendleton.[‡] Instead of

---

* Fitness Reports (FITREP): The United States Marine Corps system for evaluating the performance, character, and potential of both enlisted Marines and officers. These reports serve as a formal assessment tool, and they play a critical role in promotions, assignments, and career progression.

† Billet: A specified job or duty position within a unit.

‡ Headquarters and Headquarters Squadron, Marine Corps Air Station Camp Pendleton (H&HS Camp Pendleton): Provides logistical and administrative functions to the Air Station commander.

taking over the H&HS, I would eventually take Command of HMLA-469. All was well.

Then, things changed.

These next few paragraphs are difficult for me to write. Nothing is new to me, and I have not been shy about sharing my situation, but putting it into words for strangers to read is a step I didn't know I would take in life.

My expectations changed as I approached the promotion board for Colonel. In my earlier boards, I was never 100 percent confident but I knew I had a good chance of being promoted or selected for the jobs I wanted. I was in a similar situation as a Lieutenant Colonel: I checked all the right boxes. I had command of an HMLA, I was selected for school, and I was on my Joint Tour in EUCOM before I was on the promotion board for Colonel.

Everything was right, except for one thing. My FITREPs . . .

One of my FITREPs during my time as a Lieutenant Colonel was less than ideal; it was not going to help me get promoted. The report didn't necessarily *sound* bad. These types of reports are sometimes called "velvet daggers" because they say all the right words while placing you at a relative value well below your peers. It was frustrating to read, and only partly because of where I was ranked—the worst part was the absence of a counseling on why. Without that, I can only assume the report was designed to prevent me from getting promoted to or commanding as a Colonel.

From the moment I saw the report, I thought my chances of promotion and future Command had ended. I could see the "hole in my swing," and I knew that the next board was probably not going to go my way. My eyes were open, and I wouldn't allow myself to be surprised by bad news.

Prior to the Colonel promotion board, my boss, the Deputy J3—a one-star Marine General and infantry officer—offered to review my record.* I knew what he was going to see but I jumped at the chance to hear it from someone else. His reaction was what I expected, and his focus on my record jumped past all the good FITREPS to the one negative report. He was brutally honest with me and told me what I already knew: This report was probably going to be the reason I would *not* be selected for promotion.

He offered to help me find a way to mitigate the bad report. The Marine Corps has ways to adjudicate reports with errors, derogatory material, or reports that are seen as false. You can petition Headquarters Marine Corps through Manpower & Reserve Affairs or have your leadership, past or present, write a letter to the promotion board explaining a negative aspect of your record.

Although I was never counseled, I refused his help to mitigate the report. I told him that I wrote FITREPs on Marines for a reason and the words I wrote were deliberate. I assumed the words and rankings used by my leadership on this report were intentional and I would live and die by my record.

I can still remember the dark and damp night in Germany when I got a call from him with the Colonel promotion board results. I was sitting in our old brown recliner, about to put my son to bed. When the phone rang, I was fully prepared for him to gently give me the bad news. Instead, he told me I was selected for promotion to Colonel, and

* Record review: Similar to a more formal Career Counseling provided by Marines at Headquarters Marine Corps, a record review from a senior officer or enlisted leader scrutinizes your Fitness Reports and performance throughout your career. This highlights your strengths and weaknesses and identifies areas to improve.

Jenny and I were over the moon with excitement that our Marine Corps career would have at least one more chapter.

Colonel Command remains out of my reach. I have been looked at for Command three times, two official Command boards and one opportunity to be pulled from the alternate list into a MAG. I fell short at each opportunity. I was not surprised by the results—I knew that the less-than-favorable report held the same weight in the Command boards even as the competition with outstanding leadership from across the Marine Corps heated up. And after licking my wounds, I'm at peace with my future and happy to have served my country and the Marine Corps for as long as I have.

Too often, Marines allow themselves to be surprised when they don't get the next job or promotion. You must understand who you are, your body of work, how you have been rated, and what you know about your peers; you can't see their FITREPs, but you know the jobs they've had and how they have performed in comparison to their careers. Complete your own self-assessment: Have you had the right billets within your unit, and have you received orders to the most career-enhancing assignments? How often have you deployed, were those deployments to combat, and most importantly, what do your FITREPS say about you?

The members on your board will matter. For the members of the board, knowing you or knowing and respecting the officers who have reported on you matters. On some boards, the members can attempt to sway the vote for you but in the end, they only get one vote, and your body of work is paramount.

Be mindful of what the Marine Corps is saying to you. If you don't like it, change the Marine Corps' mind. Increase your value to the unit through hard work and dedication to your Marines, your tasks, and your leadership. If you are not in the running, you can at least get on the fence by getting assignments you need to be competitive. If you're on the fence, identify known tiebreakers to get ahead of your peers (rifle/pistol scores, PFT/CFT scores, deployments, etc.). This may seem trivial and, in most cases, will not be the deciding factor. However, if there are two Marines who have had the same jobs and similar relative values with only one spot left for Command, promotion, or selection to school, the board must find the tiebreaker, and those numbers can make the difference.

Readback

Pick your head up and look around; understand your position in life. Whether you are evaluating your relationships with family members, friends, teammates, and coworkers; applying for a promotion in your job; or striving to be selected as a Captain of your team, the world is always communicating with you. Are you listening? It's your fault if you're not! If you're on a path to success, keep working hard and stay on track to meet your goals. If you're not where you want to be, double your efforts and identify the things you can do to improve your relationships or position in life. Conduct a self-assessment, ask for advice on things you can do to improve, observe those who are succeeding in areas where you're struggling, develop a plan to achieve your goals, and take action.

CHAPTER 19

Don't Be a Talking Head

Answer the question!

When you watch an interview with a politician, you may see a masterclass in speaking without saying anything. Politicians are skilled at receiving questions and spinning a response to carry their narrative without really saying anything, even if asked a yes/no question. It can be fun to watch an interview with a politician. Often it feels like the participants are taking part in two separate conversations. This is helpful for politicians; it helps broadcast their message without being cornered into taking a real position on any topic.

It's not helpful for you. Don't do this! At least not when wearing a uniform and answering questions from senior leaders.

While in the US EUCOM J35 (Future Operations) division, I worked on many diverse and sometime complex problems. In my two years in Germany, my responsibilities included writing a

Theater Campaign Order (TCO);[*] distributing COVID-19 vaccine across the EUCOM theater; support to Turkey, Cyprus, Lebanon, and Israel; support to the Afghanistan NEO; and support to Ukraine's defense of the Russian invasion.

Many of my tasks were in support of the EUCOM Commander and Deputy Commander's engagement with senior leadership in the Joint Staff, Department of Defense, and Executive Branch. The speed at which we were operating while working on COVID vaccine distribution, the Afghanistan NEO, and Ukraine invasion far exceeded the normal battle rhythm of traditional operations in the European theater. Everyone worked together, generating products and preparing briefs at a breakneck pace.

My leadership was in constant contact with senior leaders in the US government on complex problems, and it was our job to provide solutions. I was often in the room when options were being presented, and in some cases, I was providing the options to my leadership. During confirmation briefs to the Commander or Deputy Commander, they would have detailed and often difficult questions we needed to answer. This was not the time to emulate a politician on your favorite cable news network.

The only way for a military staff officer to respond to a direct question from leadership is to "Answer the question!" The question they asked. It's tempting to answer the question you wanted them to ask or provide the response to a question you thought they might ask. Don't do it. Answer the question directly.

---

* Theater Campaign Order (TCO): A strategic document outlining US EUCOM's operational priorities, objectives, and activities within its area of responsibility.

And if you get asked a question so detailed that you don't know the answer. Say so. There is nothing wrong with telling your boss you don't know the answer and you will come back to them. This may not feel good, and it shouldn't. It's best if you know the answer, but if you don't know, say so and take it as an action item to be answered as soon as the meeting is over.

The worst thing you can do is fill the empty space created by a question for which you have no answer with an answer to a question you weren't asked. I have to be honest—I've done this, and it did not go well. It felt a lot worse than saying, "I don't know, and I will come back to you with the answer as soon as possible."

If you never know the answers to questions from your senior leaders, you are not doing your job. You'll get some very detailed questions, questions driven by the curiosity of your senior leaders or their anticipation of a question the president may ask. Learn what interests your boss and research those details to ensure you have as much information as possible prior to the brief.

Practice this in your head before beginning your brief. You may be asked a direct, single-sentence question, or you may have to decipher the intent of the question as part of a longer dialogue. The best technique is to say, "To answer your question," and then provide a response with only as much detail as is required. And then, stop talking! If your boss needs more details, they will tell you. If you've answered the question satisfactorily, you are not wasting anyone's time.

Keep track of your leadership's interests and questions they've asked during previous briefs. As you work a problem and prepare your brief, keep their interests in mind and research the topics you think they may focus on. Forecasting the questions is important and will save you from the embarrassment of saying you don't know the answer or the temptation of providing an answer to a question that was not asked.

Readback

If you aspire to be a politician or a "talking head,'" then you can say whatever you want; this chapter isn't for you. If you aspire to work well with others and accomplish difficult tasks, though, then answer the question when asked. Don't confuse a normal tendency to avoid confrontation by telling little white lies with polite answers to questions like, "Does this shirt make me look fat?"

At any job, particularly when interacting with your boss, answer questions with direct, succinct, and factual answers. Everyone knows when you're bullshitting them, and your boss will know when you don't know the answer. They may be polite and not call you out for the way you answer their questions, but they, along with everyone else in the room, will know that you may not be the one they should trust in the future.

CHAPTER 20

Sometimes Guidance Hurts

Circling the bowl.

When you're in the thick of things, getting criticized at every turn, it can be hard to recognize the wins. Like when you manage to turn several hundred sprawling pages of documentation into fifteen pages of readable, actionable guidance—as you were tasked to do—and it seems like you hear nothing but negative feedback.

This happened to me when I was a planner in the EUCOM J35 and the document in question was a TCO. This document takes strategic guidance from a Theater Campaign Plan and operationalizes the Commander's intent. The TCO directs EUCOM components to create OAIs that support a desired end state. The Theater Campaign Plan is broad in scope and the TCO provides refined guidance to subordinated commands.*

* EUCOM Components: United States Army Europe and Africa, United States Naval Forces Europe-Africa, United States Air Forces in Europe—Air Forces Africa, United States Marine Corps Forces Europe and Africa, United States Special Operations Command Europe, and United States Space Forces Europe and Africa.

Before I arrived, the TCO was hundreds of pages long, with appendixes listing thousands of tasks to subordinate commands. It was far too long, so long that very few people actually read the document. To add to the challenge, my Deputy Commander (an Army Lieutenant General) hated the TCO. Before becoming the Deputy Commander, he was the EUCOM J3 (Operations Officer) and had an in-depth knowledge of the document and what it was intended to accomplish.

Within the TCO Branch, I had a great team working for me. I put an Army Major named Adam Alexander in charge of the Operational Planning Team (OPT)* tasked with developing the next TCO. The goal was to shorten the document, refine the intent, and make it a product people would read. We were able to get it down to fifteen pages with very clear intent, removing the laundry list of specific tasks to components. But the process to get to a final product put us through a meat grinder with the Deputy Commander.

First, we had to sell him on the new concept. This was difficult not just because of his bias against the document but also because we were living in COVID times, when there were no face-to-face interactions with senior leaders. Everyone knows that in-person meetings are more productive, especially when dealing with dynamic challenges. But we had to make do with briefs that were conducted via a classified video teleconference—think Zoom for the military.

To add to the difficulty, the video teleconferences were filled with multiple heavyweight topics from across the J3. Many of the briefs would take longer than planned due to questions or guidance

* Operational Planning Team (OPT): A temporary, mission-focused group of military and interagency personnel assembled to conduct detailed planning for a specific operation or mission.

provided, and the last few briefs in the deck would become compressed based on the Deputy Commander's schedule. If you were last in line, like the TCO often was, your time to brief was reduced and so was his time to provide input and guidance.

It felt like it was a daily occurrence, but we briefed the TCO about every other week. Adam and I would tag team the briefs, with him providing the meat of the information looking down and in, and me rounding off the brief with a wider perspective looking up and out and answering questions. It seemed like we never had the right answers. It was rare for either of us to walk out of a brief feeling good. In fact, we often felt like we just walked out of a boxing match where we had our hands tied behind our backs.

To be fair, the Deputy Commander was not abusive or angry or toxic in any way. He was extremely sharp, both in his intelligence and his delivery. He didn't like what the TCO was and was shaping it, making it a better product. He had a short amount of time to hear the brief and provide his input.

The initial mission with the Deputy Commander was getting him comfortable with the new format, proving to him we could deliver more with less. We anticipated friction; after all, reducing a Combatant Command–level document from hundreds of pages to only fifteen is transformative.

Knowing we'd meet with resistance didn't prevent each interaction from stinging. No successful person, especially anyone who has spent a career in the military, enjoys continually receiving the kind of guidance that feels like a wire brushing. Some pushback is to be expected—you'd love to be able to provide a product that meets your leadership's intent on the first go, but you know that isn't realistic, especially not at the Combatant Command level.

Still, it was amazing how badly it went for me and my team at this time. The current operations division chief, a Marine Colonel and a Cobra pilot, often joked about how listening to my briefs, he felt like he was back in an HMLA sitting in on an NSI debrief where the lead instructor was dismantling the flight and calling out all the errors that needed to be corrected. He was always smiling and trying not to laugh . . . call it a sick Cobra pilot's humor.

As I looked around at the faces of my team members, I didn't see a lot of smiles—just pain.

After the meeting, though, I saw one person smiling—my boss, Colonel Joseph Kuchan, an Army infantry officer. I walked out feeling bruised and beat up, but Colonel Kuchan looked *happy*. He saw each interaction as a win. Opportunities to receive input from senior leaders were limited, especially when your boss doesn't particularly care for the product you are working on. That meant every interaction was precious. We needed guidance—we were making drastic changes to the structure of the TCO document—and we received it, even if the interactions were painful. To Colonel Kuchan, each brief was an opportunity to hear what the Deputy Commander wanted so we could update our work accordingly.

I have to admit, the process did make the product better, even if it was painful.

Colonel Kuchan referred to this process as "circling the bowl." You didn't hear me wrong; he was likening my pain and discomfort to the slow progress of a turd in a toilet as it rotates round and round the bowl. The turd doesn't go right down the moment the toilet is flushed, but every turn around the bowl brings it closer to bottom. Eventually, the process is complete. I thought he was joking the first time he said it, but he was serious. After some consideration I understood the analogy and began to embrace it.

As this concept started to settle in, it changed my perspective. It didn't soften the pain of each interaction, but it did leave me with the feeling that we were making progress. We walked into each brief with an update on the status and specific guidance we needed from the Deputy Commander. Sometimes he was happy with the direction, and we received small corrections. Other times, he was less enthusiastic, and we received larger corrections. Each interaction improved the product, and we were able to incorporate his input throughout the development of the TCO instead of being sent back to start again after we were finished. Once I realized that we walked out of each meeting feeling like we got what we needed to continue planning, I was sold on "circling the bowl."

In the end, it was a huge success. In our final brief, the Deputy Commander said, "Ryan, I love it!" Those words could not have been sweeter. The joy was short-lived, however, because—true to form—he immediately began giving guidance for how to improve on the TCO for next year. We circled the bowl for about forty-five more minutes, but every word was like gold and put us months ahead of our next planning cycle.

Readback

Don't allow guidance to make you feel like a failure. Part of any planning process includes guidance and feedback. If you aren't given clear guidance or intent at the start, the feedback loop inside the planning process is critical. Without guidance along the way, you are in danger of wasting everyone's time. If your final product isn't informed by your leadership, you may have to start again from the beginning. You should crave the guidance you need and don't allow it to set you back, even if you have to "circle the bowl."

CHAPTER 21

See Past the Obstacles

Speed bumps and roadblocks.

In any planning evolution you are going to come across unforeseen challenges and obstacles you must navigate. Some of those obstacles can be mitigated through close coordination within your staff or across external agencies. They can also be mitigated by bringing your plan to leadership for guidance or decision. I call these "speed bumps"—they slow you down, but you have direct access to the people or the individual who can approve your plan, accept the risk, and allow you to continue forward.

You'll also encounter "roadblocks"—obstacles that will stop all forward motion. A roadblock is an obstacle that you don't have the power to clear. You need someone at a very high level to take action to move forward. This is very difficult for planners to understand and accept. Some will reach a roadblock and freeze in place, assuming there is nothing more they can do until the roadblock is cleared—by someone else. This mentality will crush a planning evolution and must be avoided at all costs.

Almost any dictionary will provide a ready and useful definition for both a speed bump and a roadblock. For the purposes of this chapter, I define speed bumps and roadblocks as follows:

1. Speed bump: An obstacle across your path that causes you to slow down to navigate but can be crossed without intervention or assistance from outside entities.
2. Roadblock: A barrier across your path that impedes progress and cannot be traversed or cleared without interventions from outside entities.

Speed bumps and roadblocks are similar because they will slow or stop you from reaching your goal even though you can see past them. Although you can't move past the roadblock, you can see what the next steps will be after the roadblock is cleared. Imagine driving down a road and you come across a locked gate—the vehicle must stop, and you can't move past until someone unlocks the gate for you. You've stopped moving but you can see past the roadblock. You can see what's next; you can plan which way you will go once the gate is opened or when the roadblock is cleared.

In either case, you may not know about the obstacle until you are within a certain time or distance from it. But you can see past the obstacles to what remains ahead of you on your path. We'll focus most closely on roadblocks in this chapter.

The concept came to me while working at US EUCOM in Stuttgart, Germany. I had recently transitioned from TCO Branch Chief in the J35 to the Levant Branch Chief. In the Levant Branch I was supposed to be focused on support to countries like Israel, Lebanon, Cyprus, and Turkey. However, from 2020–2022, EUCOM attention was pulled in an assortment of other directions.

One of my tasks was to lead EUCOM's COVID-19 response, specifically the distribution of vaccine to US servicemembers and family within the European theater. In many Combatant Commands, the J35 becomes something of a junk drawer. If the problem or issue doesn't fit neatly into another directorate, it falls to the J35.

However, the work needed to be done, and by my side was a team of rock stars (Lieutenant Colonel Dave Frank (USMC), Lieutenant Colonel Neil Stark (USA), and Commander Jason "China" Pallotta (USN)) working hard to keep up with the challenges of COVID. From the White House down to the individual service members, their families, and our allies and partners. This was my first real taste of how well, and not so well, our government works with and through the military at a strategic and operational level.

As it always seemed to happen during my time in EUCOM, as soon as I was able to hand one task off—in this case, we transitioned management of COVID-19 vaccinations to the EUCOM Surgeon's office—we were handed the next hard problem. I was pulled in to help coordinate the European theater support to the Afghanistan NEO.

Our support to the Afghanistan NEO was my first experience with true strategic planning. I was able to see how senior leaders within the United States and other sovereign nations, were able to clear the way for action to be taken. As a staff officer, seeing senior leaders clear a roadblock with one phone call validated the need to continue planning past all obstacles, even when others said it would never happen.

Had we frozen in place and not planned past our roadblocks, we would have continuously remained in crisis planning mode and not been able to fully develop a deliberate, methodical, and resourced plan capable of providing options and achievable courses of action for our senior leaders. But during EUCOM's support to the Afghanistan NEO and Ukraine Crisis, I saw how one call or statement by senior leaders, Secretaries of Defense and State, and leaders of sovereign nations can clear roadblocks.

(I want to be clear—I'm very aware that anything I have to say about my experience supporting US Central Command (US CENTCOM) pales in comparison to the experience of anyone in Afghanistan, CENTCOM, and installations across the world who supported the movement and care for those individuals. I can't and won't compare the work done from the US EUCOM headquarters to the work done in any other location. That is not the point of this chapter.)

In the planning for, and execution of, support to Ukraine during Russia's invasion in 2022, for example, there was a tendency for planners at each echelon to stop planning upon reaching a roadblock. They incorrectly assumed that we would never get past the roadblock in execution of a mission, when in reality a failure to plan past the roadblock would inevitably transfer the hardest and most difficult problems down to lower echelons that were less able to solve them in a time-constrained environment. This mentality delayed the staff's forward movement with providing strategic, operational, and tactical options to our senior leaders.

The lesson here: Do not stop planning! When planning at any level, whether a Battalion or a Combatant Command, you can slow down and navigate the speed bumps. This is frustrating but it's part of the job. And, although a roadblock will stop you in your tracks, you can see past it. Look past the roadblock and identify the next challenges that need to be overcome; find the next speed bump or roadblock and identify the next major decision you will need to get from your leadership. Take action and be ready for the roadblock to be cleared by thinking ahead, knowing what needs to be done next, and leading the team to set conditions for when the path is clear again. You will have to convince, persuade, and compel others to see the way forward. Many will want to stop because it's too hard or impossible or is "never going to happen." Push those voices aside and continue. Be ready when the road is clear so you can accomplish your mission, support our allies and partners, and save—or take—lives.

Readback

Speed bumps and roadblocks are not exclusive to the military. Everyone must come up with short- and long-term plans. What to wear to an event, which way to drive to work, what to have for dinner, what college to apply to, what job field to choose, how to make a career change, how to create an emergency fund, when to get married and have a family, how to save for a vacation or buy a house . . . The list of plans we make in our daily life is endless. While planning for any of these challenges you may encounter obstacles that slow you down or stop you in your tracks. Don't stop working! Find a way to navigate the speedbumps and reach out to the people or organizations that can clear the roadblocks. Work on navigating the current obstacle with an eye down the road looking for the next challenge. With hard work, coordination, and savvy planning, you may be able to clear the next obstacle before it has a chance to slow you down.

CHAPTER 22

You're Not Being Hazed

"Higher" doesn't have all the answers.

This is very hard to hear but it is true: Your higher headquarters does *not* have the answer to every question. It is common to expect that they do, leaving you to wonder why they are not solving problems on their own, as you assume they should. This assumption couldn't be further from the truth. From a squadron or battalion to a MAG or Regiment through the Joint Staff, Office of Secretary of Defense, the National Security Council, and the White House, higher doesn't have all the answers.

I learned this while I was in US EUCOM, and the staff dealt with issues EUCOM wasn't historically accustomed to handling. What was touted as an easy tour—before arriving in Germany, anyone who knew I had orders there joked about the "wine and cheese"[*] tour I was about to begin—was definitely not. Maybe it had been true in the past, but that was not my experience at EUCOM, where I took part in the planning for and execution of the Afghanistan NEO and the United States response to Russia's invasion of Ukraine.

As the wave of tasks, Planning Orders (PLANORDs),[†] and Requests For Information (RFIs) came into the EUCOM from higher headquarters, I looked around for staff that knew the answers to the questions at hand. I had always assumed that the staff of a Combatant Command must have people who knew more than me. They must have been trained and ready to solve all of these difficult problems. But as we tasked EUCOM's components, I realized that we didn't have the answers. I had been wrong about how this worked for the entirety of my career.

When I realized that we didn't have the answers at our level, I began to look at our higher headquarters. The Joint Staff, Office of the Secretary of Defense (OSD), National Security Council, and the White House didn't have all the answers either. Each organization was made of people just like me—career government and military personnel, seasoned with endless experiences in their primary fields with multiple formal schools and degrees. But not a single person knew all the answers to the test.

---

* Wine and Cheese Tour: In recent history, orders to US EUCOM were seen as a laid-back duty station with little stress and easy access to European nations with rich culinary and cultural experiences. Orders were generally categorized as a "good deal."

† Planning Order (PLANORD): Joint Staff directive issued by the Chairman of the Joint Chiefs of Staff (CJCS) to Combatant Commanders (CCDRs) directing them to begin operational planning for a potential mission or contingency

This fact is simultaneously terrifying and what puts the US military so far ahead of its peers and competitors. It is terrifying because you have to face the fact that no one has all the answers. On the other hand, we know how to find the answers—quickly.

When higher is asking questions via RFIs and tasks you to action via PLANORDs, they need information and plans to provide information to their senior leaders—to include the president of the United States—and to make decisions. And they need it now. This is where we excel. Although chaotic and disjointed at times, the US military outpaces any other organization, to include other US governmental agencies, at planning. Each service has its own version of Joint Planning 5.0. This document takes you through each step of the planning process and allows a small group of planners to develop courses of action to accomplish any task. Our ability to start with a blank slate or shift to a new plan midstream gives us one of our greatest advantages.

Your higher headquarters can and will send endless tasks that generate more work for your people and can divert you away from what you think is most important. You might resent them for this, but you could also take it as a compliment. They don't have the answers they need, even though they, like you, are smart, hardworking staff officers doing the best they can to support a desired end state. They don't know the answers to the test. The thing is, they trust in you and your subordinate unit's expertise to get the information they need to develop a plan and make decisions. Understanding that can take a lot of sting out of the flood of tasks you get from them.

This doesn't relieve them from working hard or making hard decisions. But you must remember they have more on their plates than you do. One Combatant Command is focused on one region, but the Secretary of Defense's staff must focus on issues across all Combatant Commands.

Readback

Nobody has all the answers, in the military or in life. Not even those "above" you at work, like your boss, or even your parents. Sometimes, your role is to help those people meet the challenges that inevitably come their way. Don't assume that those with impressive job titles, degrees, or certifications know everything there is to know. They don't. And if you're working for them, you're working with them—that means that anything you can do to help them figure things out will help you both meet your goals.

Life can be difficult for people at all stages of life and across all demographics. Your boss, or your boss's boss, is a human being just like you. Do the best job you can to help your superiors to manage their requirements. If you're being asked a hard question or given a difficult task it is because you are the one with the skills, the expertise, or the time to solve a problem. Never forget that your actions can and will help others to manage their own challenges.

Conclusion

Walk around the fighting hole.

Whether you're a young Marine trying to make sense of this demanding life, a seasoned leader reflecting on how far you've come, or a civilian simply seeking to understand the mind of a service member, I hope this book has offered you something more than just a collection of stories. This has been my readback—a personal and professional deep dive, a legacy of lessons that I wish I knew before I had to live them.

I see no better way to end this book than with a perspective highlighted in a unique way during my final job as a Colonel at MARFORPAC by one of my Commanders, Lieutenant General Bill Jurney. I was his Assistant Chief of Staff (AC/S) Aviation, in charge of coordinating the implementation of Marine Corps aviation programmatic requirements and supporting the MARFORPAC staff on all aviation-related matters. Lieutenant General Jurney spoke with a North Carolina accent that could lull the unsuspecting individual into believing he was not thinking circles around everyone else in the room; he was! He also had several "Jurney-isms" he would use to drive home his guidance and intent. One of my favorites was: "Walk around the fighting hole."

Although I didn't use this term before working for Lieutenant General Jurney, I've used the sentiment for much of my life. In a military context, it means you are observing your defensive position from 360 degrees. You're looking at where you are dug in, the fighting hole, from the perspective of the enemy. Your plan may be sound from your point of view, but you also need to understand how the enemy sees you. Look at your position from the enemy's mind and strengthen any weaknesses you may have missed when developing your plan.

In life, we often fall in love with our own viewpoint. That's fine if you're always right, but those people are few and far between. I've yet to meet one. Walking around the fighting hole doesn't have to change your position; you may be on the "high ground" already. But looking at or researching the viewpoint of others makes you better. You can disagree with someone while simultaneously understanding their position and the way they view the world. This is how we should live our lives with friends and family, coworkers, political rivals, and enemies.

Walking around the fighting hole, understanding the enemy and their viewpoint, will keep your Marines alive. Understanding a family member's view of the world can lead to conflict resolution and stronger relationships. Comprehending your competitor's view in business may give you a competitive edge.

In other words, don't fall in love with your plan and who you are. Try to see the other side.

Being able to see the other side is more important than ever now, as our world seems to have become more and more polarized. If you listen to major cable and network news organizations or get fixated on narratives pushed on social media, you may feel like you are being pushed toward one side of the political spectrum or the other. Wherever you land, regardless of whether your viewpoints are shaped by pop culture or thoroughly researched options, take time to view the topic from the other side's perspective.

The best way to understand your own religious, political, or cultural beliefs is to walk around the fighting hole. If you can argue the opposing side's view on any topic, you can test them against your own beliefs—that may make them stronger, or you might find yourself changing your mind. Either way, you will better understand why you believe what you believe and why others have opposing views. People you once saw as the "opposition" will come into focus as people, people you can give grace to during challenging times. When you take the time to understand one another, to realize we are all people with our own struggles, you will realize we are all more alike than you imagined. And once you take the focus off the one thing they're doing that frustrates you, you might be able to see the good they are doing in the world.

Final Readback

As I complete my walk around this fighting hole, I find myself not just reflecting on the individual lessons forged in the crucible of my Marine Corps career, but also on the entirety of the journey. Every chapter of this book—each story, insight, and hard-earned lesson—has been a window into how I saw the world while wearing my uniform. From my earliest days navigating self-doubt and failure to being led and leading Marines in combat and crisis, this book is not about the events—it is about the perspective. My perspective. I hope I've done more than recount moments; I hope I've provided something useful, relatable, and inspirational for those who wear the uniform, once did, or wonder what it feels like to serve.

Finally, I leave these thoughts behind not as a conclusion, but as an invitation. An invitation for you to open your eyes to the challenges of life, yours and everyone around you, to lead, to learn, to live with intent—and maybe to put it in your own book.

Glossary of Acronyms and Terms (GOAT)

AC/S: Assistant Chief of Staff
ACE: Aviation Combat Element
AH-1: Attack Helicopter, model 1 – "Cobra"
AHC: Attack Helicopter Commander
AMO: Aircraft Maintenance Officer

BHR: USS Bonhomme Richard (LHD-6)
BP: Battle Position

CALA: Combat Aircraft Loading Area
CAS: Close Air Support
CASEVAC: Casualty Evacuation
CENTCOM: Central Command
CFO: Chief Financial Officer
CFT: Combat Fitness Test

CH-46: Cargo Helicopter, model 46 – "Sea Knight" or "Phrog"
CH-53: Cargo Helicopter, model 53 – "Sea Stallion"
CO: Commanding Officer
COA: Course of Action
COVID: Coronavirus disease

DACM: Defensive Air Combat Maneuvering
DAS: Deep Air Support
DC: District of Columbia
Det OIC: Detachment Officer in Charge
DFT: Deployment for Training

EUCOM: European Command

F/A-18: Fighter / Attack, model 18 – "Hornet"
F-15: Fighter, model 15 – "Eagle"
F-16: Fighter, model 16 – "Falcon"
FAC(A)I: Forward Air Control (Airborne) Instructor
FAC: Forward Air Controller
FARP: Forward Arming and Refueling Point
FCP: Functional Check Pilot
FITREPS: Fitness Reports
FOB: Forward Operating Base

GCE: Ground Command Element
GOAT: Glossary of Acronyms and Terms

H&HS: Headquarters & Headquarters Squadron
HELLFIRE: Heliborne, Laser, Fire-and-Forget
HML: HELLFIRE Missile Launcher

HMLA: Marine Light Attack Helicopter Squadron
HMT: Marine Light Attack Helicopter Training Squadron
HQMC: Headquarters Marine Corps

I MEF: First Marine Expeditionary Force
III MEF: Third Marine Expeditionary Force
ILS: Intermediate Level School
INDOPACOM: Indo-Pacific Command

J35: Future Operations Division
JP: Joint Publication
JTAC: Joint Terminal Attack Controller

LPD: Landing Platform, Dock
LSE: Landing Signalman Enlisted

MAG: Marine Aircraft Group
MAGTF: Marine Air-Ground Task Force
MANPAD: Man-Portable Air-Defense Systems
MARFORPAC: Marine Corps Forces Pacific
MATSS: Marine Aviation Training Systems Site
MAW: Marine Aircraft Wing
MAWTS-1: Marine Aviation Weapons and Tactics Squadron One
MCAS: Marine Corps Air Station
MCDP: Marine Corps Doctrinal Publication
MCOC: Marine Corps Operation Center
MEF: Marine Expeditionary Force
MEU: Marine Expeditionary Unit
MOS: Marine Occupational Specialty
MRE: Meal, Ready-to-Eat

MV-22: Multi-Mission Tiltrotor, model 22 – "Osprey"

NATOPS: Naval Aviation Training and Operating Procedures Standardization Program
NEO: Noncombatant Evacuation Operation
NSI: Night Systems Instructor
NSS: Naval Standard Score
NVGs: Night Vision Goggles

OAI: Operation, Activity, and Investment
OCS: Officer Candidate School
ODO: Operations Duty Officer
OIC: Officer in Charge
OIF: Operation Iraqi Freedom
OODA: Observe, Orient, Decide, Act
OP: Observation Post
OpsO: Operations Officer
OPT: Operational Planning Team
OSD: Office of the Secretary of Defense
OSO: Officer Selection Officer

PCS: Permanent Change of Station
PFT: Physical Fitness Test
POI: Period of Instruction
PP&O: Plans, Policies & Operations
PTO: Pilot Training Officer
PTSD: Post-traumatic Stress Disorder

RFI: Request for Information

SAM: Surface-to-Air Missile
SNA: Student Naval Aviator
SOP: Standard Operating Procedure

T-AKE: A dry cargo / ammunition ship
TBS: The Basic School
TCO: Theater Campaign Order
TIC: Troops in Contact
TLS: Top Level School
TQ: Al-Taqaddum Air Base

UDP: Unit Deployment Program
UH-1: Utility Helicopter, model 1 – "Huey"
UH-60: Utility Helicopter, model 60 – "Black Hawk"
UHC: Utility Helicopter Commander
USA: United States Army
USMC: United States Marine Corps
USN: United States Navy
USS: United States Ship

VCR: Videocassette Recorder
VT: Training Squadron

WTI: Weapons and Tactics Instructor
WWII: World War Two

XO: Executive Officer